Along Life's Way

ALONG Life's Way

Eli Landrum, Jr.

BROADMAN PRESS
Nashville, Tennessee

1981

Quotations marked RSV are from the Revised Standard Version of
the Bible, copyrighted 1946, 1952, © 1971, 1973.

Dewey Decimal Classification: 242
Subject heading: MEDITATIONS
Library of Congress Catalog Card Number: 81-66554
Printed in the United States of America

To Barbara, Leigh, and Jeff
Who have added so much love
and joy to my journey

Contents

Introduction 11

1. **"A Friend That Sticketh Closer
   Than a Brother"** 13
      J. W.'s Coat 14
      Friends 15
      Confrontation in Kindness 17
      A Familiar Voice 19
      Priest to a Pastor 21
      When Doors Slam Shut 23
      Gone Too Soon 25
      How Many Friends? 27
      The Unkindest Cut 29
2. **"As He Thinketh in His Heart"** 32
      The Sound of Hurting 32
      In Need of Grace 34
      The Need to Control 36
      Forgetting the Past 37
      Disposing of Illusions 39
      Acting on Impulse 41
      Creative Conflict 43
      Dealing with Disappointment 45
      Response to Despair 47
      What Follows Failure? 49
      Facing My Fears 52
      The Shape of Hope 54

On Being Angry. 56
Spectacular Religion. 58
3. **"The Church, . . . His Body"**. 61
From the First Day. 61
On Being the Church. 63
The Church's First Task. 65
On Being Ministry Oriented. 67
Incentive for Worship. 68
Motivation for Serious Study of Scripture. 69
On Cutting the Unemployment Rate. 71
Whose Church?. 72
The Piano Problem. 74
4. **"Bring . . . the Books"**. 77
Facing Second—or Third—Choices. 77
On Being Imperfect. 79
Lonely Fortresses. 81
The Ministry of Approving. 83
The Importance of Intercession. 85
Channeling Aggressiveness. 87
Levels of Response. 89
A Liberating Lesson. 90
Dominant Desire. 92
"Meanwhile Ministry". 94
Life's Interruptions. 96
Open to the New. 98
On Messing Up. 100
Working My Ground. 102
5. **"Out of the Mouth of Babes"**. 104
Beyond Recall. 105
When I Try. 106
What We Want, and What We Get. 108
No Going Back. 111
On Forgetting People Out. 113

Responsible for Myself. 115
The Quality of Courage. 118
"I Want to Be Like You". .119
People—or Things?. 121
The Real Truth. 123
Recapturing Wonder. 125
Getting Darked On. 127
Give Daddy Patience. 129
When We Grow Up. 130
On Liking Who We Are. .132

6.   "I Thank My God upon Every
Remembrance of You". .134
An Uncommon Man. 134
Words for the Wilderness. 139
A Lesson in Ministry. 141
A Gift of Time. 143
The Prevalence of Grief. .145
On Needing People. 147
From Unlikely Sources. 148
Persons of Worth. 150
The Power of Words. 152
A Way to Repay. 154

Introduction

Life is pilgrimage. From birth to death—and beyond, I am convinced—we journey toward a goal of the maturity we glimpse in the Crucified Carpenter who arose to offer evidence of a number of eternal truths. One of these is that life is not destined to end in dust. Instead, it moves to a different dimension which is not static but dynamic.

In our pilgrimages, none of us travels alone. From birth on, people, things, and circumstances either help or hinder us. Parents, relatives, and playmates have their input. Later, schoolteachers, classmates, church teachers, pastors, and assorted adults who are encountered in an ever-expanding world have their influences. Television, newspapers, books, records, magazines, radio—the numerous media offer materials of varying quality to our living. College or the plunge into the job market pushes back our horizons. Friends, romantic interests, then marriage partners and children share part—and often a large part—of our journey. We well *may* become a part of all we meet, and all we meet *may* become some part of us. But one thing is clear to me: We are on pilgrimage with a large company in which constant sharing takes place for good, not so good, or bad.

To this point in time, along my journey as a person, any number of people and things have contributed to what I am and to what I am becoming. I have a long way to go, but I have been helped in the past and will be assisted in the future as I make my way. In this book, I have attempted to share some of the people, books, and ideas that have provided significant points in my pilgrimage—not stopping places, but teachable moments. A word, a phrase, an act, a concept, a person—so many things have directed my thinking, and my life, along previously unexplored and challenging lines.

I am deeply grateful for the people who have seen me as a person worth their time and effort, for children—mine and others—who have taught me so much by their honest simplicity, for writers whose insights have struck responsive chords, and for friends who have accepted me as I am and have helped me to become a better person. With another man who made an infinitely more magnificent pilgrimage, I can say with honesty: "I am debtor" (Rom. 1:14). I owe a great deal to a lot of people. If this little book offers help to persons in their pilgrimages, then I will have made a small payment on my huge indebtedness.

1

"A Friend That Sticketh Closer Than a Brother"
(Proverbs 18:24)

The older I grow, the more aware I become that friendship is one of the most valuable intangibles of my journey as a person. I look back over the early stretch of my pilgrimage, and I remember a number of childhood friends. A few of these stand out as close confidants with whom I spent large segments of time. We shared frustrations, minor victories, and dreams. Others were friends to lesser degrees, boys and girls who seemed to accept me and to include me in their sometimes semiexclusive circles. Most of these I have not seen for years.

I remember several friends from my little southern Mississippi hometown who helped me make the difficult adjustment to college. Through the four years of working toward a degree, I met and formed relationships with a few of the many students attending that state institution.

Then, during a long stretch of my journey, I attended New Orleans Baptist Theological Seminary. I came away with two degrees, deep appreciation for some insightful, dedicated professors, and some basic tools for ministry. But more, I left the seminary to begin my pastoral ministry having formed some lasting relationships that time and distance have not broken. I see these relationships as among the most valuable grains of my seminary experience.

In the churches where I worked, among my colleagues in religious vocations, and now at The Sunday School Board of the Southern Baptist Convention, friends have enriched my days and made my pilgrimage easier and more enjoyable. I have learned from them, leaned on them, and let off steam as they listened. I have tried to be a friend to them, to return some of the kindnesses that I have received.

Lest I give the impression that my friends are legion, they are not. I have lost some friends. Some relationships really never developed. Some people with whom I wanted relationships in depth did not choose me. But the relatively few real friends I have are significant others for me.

J. W.'s Coat

A man that hath friends must shew himself friendly: and there is a friend that sticketh closer than a brother. (Proverbs 18:24)

An olive topcoat, it must have been bought as a light coat to ward off the chill of deep-South winter evenings or the rain for which Mobile is noted. Scores of coats just like it probably are worn in various parts of the country. More of the same color with the famous brand name may exist, but another coat like it hasn't been made—and won't be made.

The coat belonged to a friend of mine. He and his wife befriended me, and then my newlywed wife, when I was an assistant pastor on their church's staff. They took us in—into the warmth of a friendship that grew deeper with time. J. W. and Mim were older than we but young in spirit. They would call and invite us over, or provide tickets for the Senior Bowl, or make J. W.'s box at the baseball park available. And then we celebrated *the* yearly event, *the* special time: the Payne Bowl on New Year's Day, with J. W presiding and Mim keeping the concession stands stocked.

We moved away from Mobile after a while. I accepted a church in Mississippi. We got back when we could, always to an open house, open arms, and open hearts. When we couldn't get there for the Payne Bowl, or between visits, the phone would ring at some odd hour. A familiar voice on the other end of the line would inform a surprised listener that this was the IRS checking up on us. J. W. would chat for a few minutes, let us know that he and Mim were thinking about us, and get after us to come to Mobile.

We moved farther away, and visits became more infrequent. But the bond of genuine affection remained strong. J. W. and Mim came to visit us on one occasion. We went to their house in the summer on vacation.

One day the phone rang in our Alabama parsonage, and an unfamiliar voice identified herself and quickly said that J. W. had died of a heart attack. Could I come and conduct the funeral service? Shock, disbelief, anger, and grief—I felt all these in the long hours following the call. Several days later, I made the longest, loneliest trip I had made to that point in my life.

I tried to conduct the service the way I thought J. W. would have wanted it: briefly, simply, with no long eulogizing. The people who had known him needed no reminders of the quality person he was. I attempted, in my way, to pay tribute to a good friend.

Before I left Mobile, Mim gave me the coat. She wanted me to have it because J. W. would have wanted someone to enjoy it. That was his way.

Now, on cold, damp days, when I put on the coat, I think of him. I remember his generosity, his kindness, his warmth, his humor, his appreciation for life, and his love of people. In a way, the coat fits. In another way, it is much too big. I have some growing to do in order to be the man he was. J. W.'s coat reminds me that a forty regular was worn by a man of much larger spirit. And it challenges me to greater dimensions of spirit. J. W.'s coat is a friend's legacy that cannot be measured in dollars. Its incalculable worth derives from a man who lived his life well and made my life richer by who he was.

> Lord, thank you for the memories of friends who have gone on ahead in their journeys. What they were and what they gave of themselves continue to help me along my way. The models, the patterns, the challenges their lives offer to me spur me on in my attempts to stretch my life.
>
> I am grateful for people like J.W., who with warmth and generosity opened his life to me and my wife. He asked me for nothing. He gave me so much. And he had enough love to include a lot of folks. Bless his memory.
>
> In the name of the One who made befriending the nobodies of his time a priority of his ministry, Amen.

Friends

Henceforth I call you not servants; for the servant knoweth not what his lord doeth: but I have called you

*friends; for all things that I have heard of my Father I
have made known unto you. (John 15:15)*

*Thine own friend, and thy father's friend, forsake not.
(Proverbs 27:10a)*

I found the book in a little bookstore in Asheville, North Carolina.
I was browsing through the upstairs room in which the owner dis-
plays secondhand religious books, many of which are out of print
now. In the past, I had found there what to me are priceless literary
treasures. On this particular occasion, I quickly seized a fifty-year-
old volume that had been on my most-wanted list for years. I
clutched it tightly on the way down to pay for it, as though somehow it might get away from me. My eyes never left it as the owner
found the price and rang up the sale. The price of $1.75 made it
virtually a steal.

I have enjoyed reading the book. I have derived some worthwhile material for thought from it. But my mind has been drawn
repeatedly to some words written on the flyleaf of the book. Long
ago, a man gave this book to another man with this inscription:
"That this little book may be an inspiration and guide for you all
through life is the sincere wish of your friend"—and a signature in
bold strokes follows. A friend, giving something to someone else
with open, warm words of relatedness. And I thought of Arthur
Gordon's little piece on expressed love in his marvelous book, *A
Touch of Wonder*. Was the book a gift from a church member to a
pastor-become-friend? Was it from a pastor to a church member?
From a pastor to another pastor friend? Or could it have been from
one person concerned that another person, whoever he was and
whatever his role might have been, have a needed source of spiritual strength? My imagination has explored the possibilities. What
continues to impress me is that an inexpensive book bearing words
of friendship will remain a memorial of supportive care, of one
human being's unashamed affection for another person.

When I first read the inscription and reflected on it, I found myself
hoping that I had to least one friend like the one who wrote the
simple but moving and affirming words. What a source of encouragement to know that at least one person outside your family circle
cares deeply! Then, I thought again. More than having a friend like

that, I would like to *be* such a friend to those who have invited me
to share in depth in their lives.
I have been reminded that friendship is a priceless gift. Come to
think of it, the Lord of life accepted the title "Friend of Sinners,"
and he said to those who followed him, "No longer do I call you
servants, . . . but I have called you friends" (RSV). To call another
person friend and to mean it, and to be called friend by another,
with warmth and gratitude, is to be rich beyond measure.

> *Lord, accept my gratitude for those people I am priv-*
> *ileged to call friends and who call me friend. They com-*
> *prise a large part of my real wealth. Without them, my*
> *life would be much poorer.*
> *In my moments of clear, serious introspection, one of*
> *the things I want is to be a true friend ready to share in-*
> *depth in the lives of people with whom I have a special*
> *relationship. Never let me lose a sense of the supreme*
> *value of friendships which make my journey easier and*
> *more pleasant.*
> *Thank you most of all for your friendship.*
> *In the name of him who offers his redemptive friend-*
> *ship to every person, Amen.*

Confrontation in Kindness

Faithful are the wounds of a friend; but the kisses of an
enemy are deceitful. (Proverbs 27:6)

I went a long time without understanding the place of confrontation in friendship. Then, quite unexpectedly, I was confronted in
kindness by a friend who helped me to make one of many beginnings, one of many tentative steps, in my journey as a person.
I had met him as one of a large number of beginning students in
the seminary. He had come to New Orleans from Alabama. I had
come from Mississippi. Our relationship was casual for a while.
Gradually it grew into a friendship marked by mutual respect, acceptance, and sharing. We became roommates. I moved from
undergraduate study into graduate school. He received his under-

graduate degree and entered a pastoral clinical psychology program at Baptist Hospital. And, sometimes with a lot of mutual support, we worked toward our goals.

One day, we were in our dorm room. I was shaving, and he was
reading. We were talking about dating—and, in particular, some of
the girls who were prime candidates for our attention. I don't recall
the girl's name now, but I mentioned a young lady whom I wanted
to date.

"If I had some indication that she would accept, I'd ask her out," I
said.

He just looked at me for a long moment. Then he said, "You
know, roomy, that's something I've noticed about you. In just about
everything you do, you have to have an edge."

I remember being surprised and a little irritated that he would
point out a flaw in what I tried hard to present as a got-it-together
personality. I responded: "No, that's not true. I don't have to have
an edge."

"Yes, you do," he continued. "You always have to have an
advantage. Take dating, for instance. You don't take a chance like
the rest of us do. You don't ask unless you have an indication that
the girl will say yes. You're going to have to take your chances with
the rest of us."

Again, I denied the charge. We talked on for a few minutes and
then moved to another subject, much to my relief. Later, I thought
about the exchange. Forced into some honest looking at myself, I
had to admit that he was right. I did look for the advantage, the
edge. Why was I so special that I had to approach the aspects of my
life with the jump on others? I began to look at myself and my
approach to people and things in a little different manner.

It was a small step, but it was a beginning, my conversation with a
friend. Only years later did I learn the correct terminology for what
had happened in that dorm room. A friend had confronted me in
kindness. He had shown me something about myself that I did not
want to see. In fact, I had refused to see at first and well may have
gone on with the blind spot in my makeup had it not been for him.

I have been helped to see some other things about myself that I
continue to work on. But I look back to a moment in time when a
friend thought enough of me to confront me and to start me toward
self-understanding. Real friendship has a place for confrontation—

not in anger, or in an attempt at one-upmanship, or in an attitude of superiority—but in care.

> *Lord, looking back, I am grateful for those friends who made me look at some unpleasant truths about myself. I wasn't thankful when the experiences took place. Sometimes, I was angry in my denials. But some people back there, with care and tact, ran the risk of offending me in order to help me. I appreciate them more now.*
>
> *Help me to be able to seize the right moments to confront friends in kindness—with a definite emphasis on kindness. I don't want to confront others in anger or in glee at flaws in their makeup. Help me to care enough to run the necessary risks to be more than a yes-friend.*
>
> *In the name of the One who helped people to see the truth about themselves and who always did it in love, Amen.*

A Familiar Voice

A friend loveth at all times, and a brother is born for adversity. (Proverbs 17:17)

As I recall now, looking back over the intervening years, the incident occurred on a Saturday morning. A lot had happened in the days immediately prior to that Saturday. I was an intern assistant to the pastor on the staff of a large church. During a Wednesday evening session over which I was presiding, one of the church's leaders had read the pastor's resignation and intention to retire. I was caught completely off-guard. It was one of the many times in my life that I have been hit from the blind side. I had had no indication of what was coming.

Following the shocking announcement, I was told that I was to preach the following Sunday. This left three days to prepare two sermons—not nearly enough time, I thought. Not for me, anyway. And I felt tremendous pressure. Then, after a while, another thought surfaced: I now was the only pastoral minister to that huge congregation. For someone as green as I was, who had come to learn something about ministering in a Baptist church, the experience was timber-shaking, to understate the feeling by a long way.

On the morning still vivid in my memory, the phone rang in the bedroom of our small apartment. On the other end of the line, a familiar voice greeted me and identified himself as though identification were necessary. He and I had grown up together in the same small, south Mississippi town. We had spent some time together in college and seminary. Now, he was on the staff of a large church in Florida. He had heard of the situation in my church.

"What does this mean for you?" he asked. "Are you and Barbara all right?"

I assured him that as far as I could tell, my job was secure. I had no indication that any move was under way to "clean house"—although, as I had learned just recently, things do sneak up unannounced. We talked for a few minutes and hung up. And I reflected on his call. I had a warm feeling at the thought that a friend cared enough to call and ask how I was doing in a difficult circumstance. He had wanted to know if he could do anything. He had taken the time, made the effort, and communicated care. I felt encouraged and supported, and a bond of friendship was made stronger.

Years later, I learned that a friend in another state was making a pastoral move. Earlier, he and I had shared the pressures we felt in our pastorates—pressures that would not allow us to minister as effectively as we would like, pressures that affected our families. I was happy that he had received an opportunity to minister in another place. Then I remembered my friend's call years before and what it had meant to me in a time of rapid change. I called my pastor friend and former seminary classmate. My wife and I talked with him and his wife about their move and how they felt about it. We hoped that our act of calling conveyed the sincere care we felt—the kind of care that an earlier call had communicated to us.

The Saturday morning call years ago taught me a valuable lesson: No matter how much distance separates friends, we have ways to reach across the miles with concern. One such way is the sound of a familiar voice saying, "I care." When that happens, one friend ministers to another friend on a level that almost defies description. And, after all, that is at least part of what friends are for.

Lord, thank you for friends who care. Some have given so much of themselves to me and have received too little from me. Some now reach out to me in kindness, making my way easier by allowing me to be myself, by offering themselves in my trouble spots and rough stretches, by challenging me with the quality of their lives. Bless them for running the risk of extending friendship.

In the name of the One who offered—and goes on offering—his friendship to the friendless, Amen.

Priest to a Pastor

Unto him that . . . hath made us kings and priests unto God and his Father; to him be glory and dominion for ever and ever. Amen. (Revelation 1:5b-6)

But ye are a . . . royal priesthood. (1 Peter 2:9)

She was well into her seventies, but I never could view her as being her age. She was in excellent health, energetic, and always doing something—often for other people. She was active in her church, much more active than any number of people half her age. I enjoyed the privilege of being her pastor for over six years. I enjoyed her support, and I attempted to minister to her in crises that came. She helped me consistently by making me aware of needs she found among the church membership.

At one point in my ministry, I faced a crisis. A number of factors had merged to create a pressure-packed situation for me. On a Sunday night, after the evening worship period, the chairman of deacons had dropped by my office to say that we would have a called deacons' meeting the next night "to talk about the shape of the church." I didn't have to be a genius to catch the unspoken threat underneath his words: The pastor was to be put in the dock. I was going to be straightened out—or worse, sent on my way. My anxiety cleared the top of the scale in no time at all. Later that night, I found out that my interpretation was right on target. The tension-filled hours of Monday dragged slowly toward zero hour. I made what preparation I could and waited.

Late in the afternoon of The Meeting, I was too nervous to be still, so I left the church office, got into my car, and started to drive around aimlessly. I realized that I literally had no place to go. No place existed that could offer refuge or escape from the inevitable moment. After just a few minutes and a short distance, I headed home to wait out the hours with my wife.

When I arrived at the pastorium, a familiar car was parked in front. My kind, supportive lady was sitting in the kitchen, sharing my wife's anguished moments. She stayed for a while after I got there, listening a lot, talking some, giving support by her presence and open care.

I had read of one person's sudden realization that she had been priested by a neighbor. I had used her words in a sermon whose theme is that we can be—we must be—priests to each other. Now, a church member who had become a friend had entered our storm to share our experience. In acceptance and understanding, she allowed us to express our anxiety, frustration, and anger. Some church members would not have liked her supporting us. But she came to let us know that we could count on her friendship and to allow us to verbalize some of the pain.

She knew what many of us discover when we attempt to minister to people who are in crisis, who are hurting: Sometimes all you can do is to go to another person and stand beside him or her. Words sometimes become inadequate, unnecessary. The presence—the being there—speaks eloquently of one person's care for another.

I was her pastor, but at a crisis point in my journey she became my priest. I never will forget her.

Lord, I know what having someone act as my priest means. She represented you to me when I needed care to wear a human face. She shared my hurt. Help me to be more willing to be a priest to others, to have the courage to share their pain.

In the name of the One who shares our hurt at a depth that I cannot know, Amen.

When Doors Slam Shut

Ointment and perfume rejoice the heart: so doth the sweetness of a man's friend by hearty counsel. (Proverbs 27:9)

She is tall, slim, and plainspoken. But unlike many people who pride themselves on shooting straight from the shoulder verbally, she also will listen. And she cares deeply about people.

My first encounter of substance with her was in a crisis situation in which she expressed her care. Late one evening, she called me from a Mobile hospital. I was the assistant pastor on the church's staff, but the church was without a pastor at the time, so I was on call. Two young ladies on their way to her house for a Sunday School class meeting had been involved in a serious accident. Their car had been plowed into by a drunken driver in a car larger and heavier than theirs. One of them was injured critically. Would I come to speak with the injured woman's husband? I rushed to the hospital and spent some time with the distraught young man, but the caring lady was the one who ministered most effectively. During the long days, weeks, and months that went by while the young woman struggled back from the edge of death, my straightforward lady (who was to become a dear friend) was more than a Sunday School teacher to the young woman. She was friend, minister, companion, and protector. My respect and admiration for this unique, lovely person grew.

The friendship between our families continued to develop, mainly because the lady reached out to my wife and me with warmth and openness. We grew to love her and her family. I valued opportunities to talk with her, to listen to her opinions, to ask her advice, to learn from the varied experiences that she had had while working in churches.

On one occasion, I sought her sympathy. Of all the people I knew, I thought that she would understand how I felt. I had had a jarring experience that left me shaken. I had visited a family in order to invite them to visit our fellowship in Bible study or worship and, hopefully, to become part of our church. I drove to the house, walked up on the porch, and knocked on the glass door. A young wife, followed closely by a curious toddler, came to the door. I introduced myself and expressed my church's interest in her and her family. She answered that they didn't go to church much. I repeated my invitation for them to visit our church. At least, I was in the process of doing so when a look of stark rage clouded and distorted her face. She shoved her child out of the way and slammed the wooden door in my face.

To this day, I find that I cannot describe what I felt in that moment and for some time to come. I felt what must have been humiliation. It was something more than embarrassment. And I became deeply angry. I was hurt. I never had had a door slammed in my face in anger.

For a few days, I licked my wound. Then, I had a chance to tell my friend-adviser-confidante about my experience. And I really expected sympathy to soothe my bruised feelings. Instead, I received something I needed more from a friend who minced no words.

First, she smiled. Then she laughed. She actually laughed! Evidently amused at how seriously I was taking myself and the incident of the door, she said: "Why, honey, that isn't anything. You haven't run into anger and coldness until you have knocked on doors in . . . (a state in the northeast). I can't count the number of doors I have had slammed in my face. If that were going to stop me, I'd have quit a long time ago. But a door slammed in my face isn't about to discourage me."

I must have stood there with my mouth open. I guess I had expected words or gestures to fuel my self-pity. What I received was a needed jolt, a verbal shake to jar me out of my overattention to my sensitive feelings. Of course, she was right. A door slammed in your face is a pretty fair gesture of rejection. But you can expect this experience to be repeated in life. Some folks are not going to let you into their houses or into their lives. In any number of ways, they will slam doors in your face. *But what you can do is to go on to the next person* with your offer of interest and care.

As I look back, I think what my good friend was trying to say was that *our responsibility as persons and as Christians is to offer ourselves.* When the doors are slammed in our faces, responsibility has shifted. I try to remember that as I go on encountering people in my pilgrimage—and as some doors being slammed shut cut me off in mid-word or mid-gesture.

Lord, I don't like to be rejected. Something deep inside longs to be liked and accepted by all the people I meet. Intellectually, I know that this is impossible. Emotionally, I have difficulty accepting the cold, hard fact that for the rest of my life, I will have to deal with rejection. Help me to cope with it with some measure of maturity.

Thank you for the gracious friend who taught me that I can take myself so seriously that I turn small hurts into gaping wounds. Help me to learn from every jolt life hands me, and allow me to laugh at myself at times and go on with my living.

In the name of him who knew ultimate rejection and still loves, Amen.

Gone Too Soon

For who shall have pity upon thee, O Jerusalem? or who shall bemoan thee? or who shall go aside to ask how thou doest?. . . . She that hath borne seven languisheth: she hath given up the ghost; her sun is gone down while it was yet day. (Jeremiah 15:5,9a)

On one of his albums, Neil Diamond sings a song entitled "Done Too Soon." In his song, he has written about a number of people who came on history's scene, made their contributions—good and bad—and then left the stage too soon. The implication is that had they not been cut off, they would have done even more. And Diamond hints hauntingly that we all will be done too soon.

In Jeremiah 15, God through his prophet described Judah's fate in dramatic, poetic language: "Her sun is gone down while it was yet day." Although Judah's sun had set before day was over because of her rebellion against God, the striking phrase reminds me of people who, through no fault of their own, had their suns to set in the middle of life's day.

He had done undergraduate study at another seminary and had come to the seminary in New Orleans to do graduate work. That first summer he, another undergraduate student, and I spent a great deal of time together. We ate some meals together, and we "bummed around" some—usually in his car, since he was the only one of us who owned one. His hobby was photography, and he was extremely good at it. He had a terrific sense of humor. His jokes never took advantage of other people; he was never funny at anybody else's expense. He became pastor of a small rural church and gave some of us opportunities to preach. Throughout graduate school, he was a popular, personable, capable student and friend. We never were the closest of friends, but I appreciated the relationship. We finished school and went separate ways, and I kind of lost track of him. I only saw him at conventions now and then, and we renewed the acquaintance.

A few years ago, the shocking news came: This quality person and pastor had died of leukemia. He was gone too soon; his sun had gone down in the middle of his day. And I grieved for him—and for myself, because I was reminded vividly of the thin string by which my life and others' lives hang.

Every now and then the reports come: the terminal illness of a high school classmate; a heart attack that claimed a seminary acquaintance; an automobile accident that took the life of a man I grew up with, my age; a car crash that killed another seminary classmate. All of them were cut off in the middle of life, with so much more to do, to offer. And something in me recoils at the seeming unfairness of people's going too soon.

But I think of the seminary friend, and I remember his contributions to the lives of those who knew him and of those to whom he ministered. And I am impressed again with the truth that his life and other lives like his teach: It is not how long we live but how well. It is not the number of our years but the quality of those years. And I am motivated to work at filling my years.

Lord, thank you for the lives of friends who have gone too soon. At least, as far as I can determine their lives were terminated early. Some of these people lived so well during their all-too-brief lifetimes that their mem-

ories continue to challenge me. They added something intangible to my journey, and I am grateful for the brief encounters between their lives and mine.

Help me to live well, Lord, so that I make good use of my time in this life in order that I may be able to give something of worth to the people I meet. Keep me from taking days and years for granted, for whatever time I have remaining will be a gift from you. Help me to receive my days gratefully and to live them responsibly.

In the name of the One who had his life cut off while he was in his prime, Amen.

How Many Friends?

A man that hath friends must shew himself friendly: and there is a friend that sticketh closer than a brother.
(Proverbs 18:24)

He had been retired from the pastorate and denominational work for a number of years. At seventy-five, he still was active and mentally sharp, a good preacher with something to say. He was serving as interim pastor of the church where I worked as a part-time staff member. On this particular Wednesday night, he was teaching from Paul's letter of Philemon. He was discussing friendship. Suddenly, he asked how many friends each of us had. If he asked for a verbal accounting, how many true friends could we count on? He defined a genuine friend: one to whom we could go at any time with any matter, with whom we could be ourselves, and by whom we could count on being accepted, heard, and helped. After a short pause, he said that he was going to tell us how many good, intimate friends he had. I honestly thought that he was going to indicate a large number. Slowly, he held up two fingers. Two men who had been friends of his across the years were the ones he could share anything with in trust and comfort. Of course, he had a much larger number of friends, but two friends were the intimate, caring, supportive, and completely open kind.

I began to think about what he had said. How many real friends did *I* have, people I could trust with deepest thoughts and feelings, people I could count on, people with whom no masks were necessary or possible? The number is not as large as I would like to think or claim. I have an idea that if I have more than two, I am most fortunate.

I have read somewhere—and have preached—that if we have a half-dozen people outside our immediate families who really care about us, we are fortunate. Now I think that my figure was too high. I have an idea that most of us have many acquaintances or contacts—and few real friends.

The older I grow, the more convinced I become that one of the most important and valuable factors in my living is friendship. Sharing on a deep level with people outside my family who know me for who I am and accept me with all my flaws is a matchless privilege that I cannot take lightly. I can't choose to relate closely to everybody; I don't have the capacity—or the inclination—to be open completely to all the people I meet. But I do want a number of people who will tell me honestly how they see me and my actions, and who will insist that I be honest with them and with myself.

This coin has another side. I hope that when some people with whom I have shared and now share my journey count their real friends, they can list me as one who cares about them, one who is part of their meaningful minority.

> *Lord, I am grateful for those few people outside my family circle who know me well and accept me anyway. They listen well and advise little. They support without patronizing. They give without strings attached. They help me to see the truth about myself without being harsh. They care. Help me to return the openness and warmth of my meaningful minority. Help me to listen to them and feel with them. I want to be able to laugh with them when they celebrate success and victory. I want to be able to weep with them when they grieve. Only you can make me more compassionate than I am to those who look on me as a friend. Please go on working at it.*
>
> *In the name of him who had few friends but is Friend to many, Amen.*

The Unkindest Cut

Yea, mine own familiar friend, in whom I trusted, which did eat of my bread, hath lifted up his heel against me (Psalm 41:9)

And immediately, while he yet spake, cometh Judas, one of the twelve, and with him a great multitude with swords and staves, from the chief priests and the scribes and the elders. And he that betrayed him had given them a token, saying, Whomsoever I shall kiss, that same is he; take him, and lead him away safely. And as soon as he was come, he goeth straightway to him, and saith, Master, Master; and kissed him. And they laid their hands on him, and took him. (Mark 14:43-46)

You expect it from your enemies—those who oppose you, dislike you in varying degrees, or outright despise you. You know that those who have it in for you, for whatever reasons, will put you down when they can. They will shadow your reputation and integrity with doubt. They will do their best to take your name. Some will put whatever pressures they can on you—financial, social, and political. They will attempt to isolate you, even from your friends. They will level you if they can. We all have our detractors, our opponents.

But when a friend turns on you, you are presented with a searing cut that is difficult to cope with. The psalmist was trying to deal with the defection of a "familiar friend" whom he had trusted and who ate his bread. Evidently, an intimate friend had turned on the puzzled, hurt psalmist. What hurt goes deeper than that caused by a friend-become-enemy? We choose a few people to share our secrets, to be entrusted with guarded thoughts and feelings that we dare not share wholesale. We share meaningful time and significant table fellowship with a small number of carefully selected intimates. When one who has shared such secrets, quality time, and meals which are offerings of friendship sells us out, it is a large and bitter pill to swallow.

Only in the last few years have I reached a deeper understanding of Jesus' agony in the garden of Gethsemane. I never will plumb the depths of his pain, for his was a one-of-a-kind experience, unique and never to be repeated. But I appreciate it more now. Part of his deep anguish was caused by the defection of one who had been with him. Judas had shared Jesus' deepest thoughts. He had had the opportunity to spend quality time with Jesus. He had shared numerous meals with his Master. At the Last Supper, Jesus had made repeated overtures to Judas. He had offered his redemptive friendship in every way that he could. Yet, Judas was the one who made it possible for the religious leaders to seize Jesus at an opportune time and in a place away from the crowds. And I cannot know the pain that Jesus felt as Judas kissed him to identify him for the mob. A friend had "lifted up his heel" against Jesus and had turned friendship into a mocking satire.

To a much lesser degree, to be sure, the psalmist's and Jesus' experiences came to me at one critical point in my pilgrimage. I still am attempting to work my way through it so that no emotions of anger are stirred when I recall what took place. I had thought that we were friends—if not bosom buddies or best friends, at least two men who had shared time, food (his and mine), and thoughts. I felt that we understood each other pretty well. Every pastor needs someone, inside or outside his church, in whom he can confide— someone in whose presence he can relax and be himself. In fact, every individual, no matter what his or her role or work, needs such a person. He was one of those. I trusted him.

Shortly before I moved from the church, I began to get indications that I no longer had his full support. In the face of mounting pressure put on me by some in the congregation, I held stubbornly to the conviction that he would stand with me if I faced ultimate crisis. Then, I insisted in the face of my growing doubts about him that at least he would be fair. It was not until some months after I had resigned as pastor that I learned exactly how far down the river he had sold me. When I learned the truth, I was disappointed and angry. I still am. Friends don't turn on friends when the chips are down. And they don't leave them in the pit alone, not if at any point the friendship was more than surface courtesies.

Something good has come out of what has been a difficult experience. I am more determined than ever to run risks in order to be as supportive as I can be to some who call me friend. I don't lead the league in number of friends or in degree of courage, but I would like to be a man of integrity in friendships, one on whom a few others can count—in calm and in storm.

Lord, I am struggling with your demand that I forgive. I know the Scripture references. I realize that you have forgiven me for infinitely more than anything anybody could do to me. Forgiveness once was easy for me, when the hurts were slight. But then the big blows landed; the cuts were deep and painful. The scars remain. And now I know just how difficult forgiveness is sometimes, how costly it can be. Help me to forgive the bailing out of one I looked on as a friend. Go on teaching me lessons for my living out of that disturbing experience. Most of all, enable me to be a loyal friend.

In the name of the Friend who never lets his friends down, Amen.

2

"As He Thinketh in His Heart, So Is He"
(Proverbs 23:7)

Because none of us is an island or lives in a vacuum, other people impact our lives, make impressions on us, and stimulate our thinking. What we hear, see, read, and feel opens up new avenues of deliberation for us. We are prompted to think about our own lives, our relationships with other persons, our privileges and responsibilities, our world and our purpose in it. We are helped to examine and deal with our feelings. In the secret citadels of our lives, we do the thinking out of which we live.

The thoughts which I share in the following vignettes have come out of what I have experienced. Many of the deliberations were sparked by the questions, responses, and sharing of people whose lives touched mine. Some of my thinking was done in crisis, in searing personal pain. I am indebted to those individuals who helped me, and forced me, to do some serious thinking about many of the things that really matter in life.

The Sound of Hurting

My God, my God, why hast thou forsaken me? Why art thou so far from helping me, and from the words of my roaring? O my God, I cry in the daytime, but thou hearest not; and in the night season, and am not silent. (Psalm 22:1-2)

My heart is sore pained within me: and the terrors of death are fallen upon me. Fearfulness and trembling are come upon me, and horror hath overwhelmed me. And I said, Oh that I had wings like a dove! For then would I fly away, and be at rest. (Psalm 55:4-6)

Sometimes, when I listen closely, I can hear it. Too often, I choose not to listen; but even at that, I go on being surprised at the frequency with which I recognize it. The quiet undertone of pain throbs in words that come with difficulty, probing tentatively for the understanding which will allow expressions of feelings to flow freely. I am amazed constantly at the new dimensions of real suffering that I am discovering when I really listen to people. I have hurt; I have experienced something of the depth of agony as cutting as any physical pain I have felt. But I have not touched bottom yet. I have come close, but I have not been there. I am hearing people who have been there, who are there now, who want and need some help toward healing.

The sounds that I hear are not chronic complaints about imagined slights or minor injuries to hyperdelicate feelings. Hopefully, I am learning to tune out those who broadcast their nurtured irritations, who wear their feelings on their sleeves so that they are bumped and bruised easily and often. I am having less and less time for patting, pacifying, and soothing pseudovictims. They need help, too; and moments may come when they can be put in touch with where they are in their living, and why they are there. But I am fresh out of patience with those who demand emergency-room attention to minor problems while others struggle silently and courageously with deep, searing wounds.

We have a choice concerning the real hurt we encounter in life. Out of our experience of pain, we can extend understanding, empathy, and support to people stunned by one of life's blows. Or, we can add blows of our own. We can be people who inflict pain, who carelessly or maliciously injure and maim out of our anger, insecurity, jealousy, or insensitivity. We can be people who help to heal or who wound.

A church should be a fellowship of persons who can hear the sounds of hurting—persons who share their hurt in an atmosphere of trust and who move to heal the hurt they recognize in daily encounters with their fellows. I have begun to wonder why so many people go outside our churches for attention to their wounds. They will go where they can find care, where their real needs are met.

A person who is serious in following Christ will make the effort to hear as Christ heard. In order to gain a hearing for the good news, Christ's person first may have to listen—to people who identify with the psalmist who asked why God had left him and with the psalmist who longed for the ability to fly away from his pain, to escape. One thing is certain: People who are hurting are going to find people— or a person—who will hear and feel their pain.

We are tuned in to a variety of things around us. I wonder how often we hear—how much we really want to hear—the soft sound of hurting.

> *Lord, I have hurt; and I have talked to you about it. I have not always heard your reply, but I knew that you care. I know what it is to feel physical, mental, and emotional anguish. Sometimes, inside, I have screamed in helpless rage against my hurt and its cause. But I know others whose pain is more intense than mine ever has been. Help me to be willing to hear them when they try to express their loneliness, their grief, their guilt, their hopelessness, their inner emptiness, their throbbing physical pain which cripples their whole lives. Help me to have the courage to risk feeling a part of what they experience. At this point in my life, I am blessed with minimal difficulty. Help me not to forget or ignore those who travel through dark tunnels of pain and who see no light ahead.*
>
> *In the name of the One who was infinitely sensitive to the hurts of the humanity he encountered, Amen.*

In Need of Grace

> *Therefore being justified by faith, we have peace with God through our Lord Jesus Christ: by whom also we have access by faith into this grace wherein we stand. (Romans 5:1-2)*
>
> *But where sin abounded, grace did much more abound. (Romans 5:20)*
>
> *We then, as workers together with him, beseech you also*

that ye receive not the grace of God in vain. (2 Corin-
thians 6:1)

Deep down inside, I had known it all along. I had read it and
heard it and had agreed that the words applied to me, not to someone else who was handy. I had preached it repeatedly. But somehow, in the course of group interchange, when the incisive, caring
person said it again, it registered as never before.

"We are all people who are in need of grace," the hospital chap-
lain said emphatically. "Ultimately, we must look to God's grace."

The context of the statement was not religious, but deeply
human. Five pastors with various hurts were seated in the chap-
lain's office as he led us to look at ourselves and our work. And we
were trying to deal with our "stuff" as honestly as we could. We
struggled to get handles on some perplexing problems in our ministries and in our personal lives. We were being reminded that the
most critical need of all persons is the need of grace. In that
moment, I saw it as my deepest need.

If I can grasp this truth and hold on to it, it can do some good
things for me. It can prevent me from thinking more highly of
myself than I ought, as Paul put it so well. My awareness of my
need of grace can keep me from being guilty of spiritual arrogance.
The truth that *I* need grace daily can get me in touch with the
common ground on which I stand with people I can see as brothers
and sisters. I share something with other people I encounter—
people with whom I relate or with whom I clash. We have a point of
real relatedness—grace from outside ourselves which comes as
pure gift. This realization can move me to a healthy tolerance of
others. It can make me more hesitant to judge and dismiss quickly,
less hasty to criticize and to demean, more disposed to extend
grace.

Paul knew something that I need to be reminded of constantly:
Grace is given to be passed on, to be shared. For, unless I share
God's lavish grace, I receive that grace in vain, to emptiness; I frus-
trate the grace of God. The thought sobers and shakes me: I can
stymie the grace of God by refusing or neglecting to be gracious.

Lord, help me never to take your grace lightly or for
granted. May I not be guilty of trying to keep your grace

*to myself and thus frustrating it and emptying it. Show
me how to share your grace with those whose lives touch
mine.*

*In the name of the One who put a human face on
grace, Amen.*

The Need to Control

*For God hath not given us the spirit of fear; but of power,
and of love, and of a sound mind. (2 Timothy 1:7)*

The need is in all of us, to some degree. We gain a distinct
advantage when we recognize it and deal with it in such a way that
we grant to ourselves and to other persons the freedom to be as we
are. Each of us has, to a great or small or somewhere-in-between
degree, a need to control other people.

Many marriages are reduced to grim games in which a partner
maneuvers to control the other. One seeks to become dominant,
calling the shots, and shaping the image of the other. Sometimes,
children become pawns in the game. They comprise a ready audi-
ence for marital put-downs, or they are used to convey messages.

The struggle to control can be observed in friendships, busi-
nesses, and social groups. The desire—the need—to control is a
powerful drive.

As a pastor, I became aware that those in the pastoral ministry
usually have a strong need to control. They need to control persons
and committees and programs so that things go as projected. To
the degree that pastors take seriously the personalities, individ-
uality, and creativity of other people, to that degree they free themselves from anxious manipulating, from frantic clutching of the
reins. Pastors then can allow—can enable—other persons to
assume responsibility and to suggest where they would like to go as
a church.

On the other hand, some church folks bring to their involvement
in their church a great need to control. They can't control their
marriage partners, their children, the demands of their jobs, or the
rapidly rising cost of living. But in the democratic, spiritual setting of
the church, where a strong desire for peace usually exists, where

the tendency to placate is evident, and where anxiety levels are raised easily and quickly—a person can exercise some control. And many people set out to do just that. They try to control the pastor by outlining his image and charting his work for him. And budget-adoption time always offers a chance to apply the leverage of finances to one totally dependent on the church for his livelihood. Some people attempt to control committees so that their ego-stroking suggestions become policy, procedure, or program. And a few people try to control deacons or other persons in leadership by some well placed, not so subtle "a good deacon (leader) would . . . " hints.

Most of us need to exercise one kind of control consistently. The King James Version translates the word as "a sound mind," one meaning of the term. The word can mean self-control. The term is suggestive. I have me to control, and I am finding that that task takes most of my time and energy. Maybe with self-control, control of other persons won't be necessary—or desirable.

Lord, grant me the grace to allow others to be free in my presence. Help me to resist the temptation to attempt to manipulate other people. Help me to listen, to weigh what is said, and then to change my stance if I need to do so. May I look at those in my path as persons, not as objects. Help me never to reduce other people to less than they are in your sight by my viewing them as things to control so that I can have my way.

In the name of the One who treated everyone as a person to be loved and who freed them in his presence, Amen.

Forgetting the Past

Brethren, I count not myself to have apprehended: but this one thing I do, forgetting those things which are behind, and reaching forth unto those things which are before, I press toward the mark for the prize of the high calling of God in Christ Jesus. (Philippians 3:13-14)

He stopped me in one of the church hallways. He was serious about his participation in his church. He was extremely active, and he was a leader. We stepped to one side, out of the flow of people. In hushed tones, he said: "I want to give you a topic to write on."

"What do you have in mind?" I asked, waiting warily for the other shoe to drop. I half expected to be ribbed good-naturedly about my column in the church paper.

"Write an article on putting hurts in the past," he replied seriously. "Our Sunday School lesson today included Paul's words about forgetting the past. Tell us how to do it."

"I'm not at all sure that I have an answer," I responded, wishing fervently that Paul had told us how to erase the unpleasant, bitter experiences of our yesterdays. "In fact," I said, laughing nervously, "I'm sure I don't have an answer. But I'll think about it."

I did think about it, and I didn't come up with a simple, surefire answer. How *do* you forget the past, or can you? Can a person put past disagreements and wounds where they belong—in the past, with no negative effect on the present? Can an individual put past successes behind instead of trying to polish the glory constantly—missing today's opportunities in the process?

If by the phrase, "forgetting those things which are behind," Paul meant simply blotting from memory experiences—good and bad—then his words have no meaning for me. I want to remember some of the good things. Sometimes, I recall one of them and treasure it for a few moments. Such memories have given light and warmth on some dreary days. And I can't forget some of the painful experiences. The hurt was too intense, the impression too indelible. Some things refuse to be erased completely.

But if Paul meant that he had worked through positive and negative experiences—especially those that had hurt—so that they no longer disrupted or emptied the present for him, then he says a great deal to me. If my past—good and bad—causes me to live there instead of in the now, then my past empties my present. I can build on the past; I can't live there.

One way that we can begin to put our hurts behind us is to allow a trusted friend to priest us. We can express our pain to a person who can support or confront us as needed. Sometimes, when hurt is expressed to someone who cares and who can be objective, it loses some of its sharpness. Somehow, it doesn't smart quite as much. We can be helped to look at the wound, to work our way through the pain, and to have our hurt understood by a significant other person. Then the hurt is dulled, at least a little.

In addition, we can stop nurturing our hurts. For some people, feeling hurt is a favorite feeling. Somebody else is to blame for their not feeling good about themselves and about life in general. They keep the wounds sensitive—and on display. If we constantly call up our hurts and nurture them, they will go on poisoning the present. We have the option of letting go of our hurts, of refusing to keep a sore spot sensitive, and of allowing a wound to close.

Finally, we can put hurts behind by focusing our efforts on worthwhile goals. We can work to be better persons, better marriage partners, better parents, and better followers of Christ. When mental and emotional energy is spent on a positive goal, we have neither the time nor the inclination to spend time on the past, making sure that wounds do not heal.

All of us have scars, near the surface of our living or deep down inside. But none of us has to walk around with open emotional wounds—unless we want to do so.

> *Lord, help me to use my yesterdays instead of being held captive by them. Help me to "let bygones be bygones," as my parents used to put it. Give me the determination necessary to let old hurts die. I have today and an undetermined number of tomorrows. Help me not to waste them fruitlessly on a past that I cannot change. I want to fill today full. I want to be effective and productive all my days. Help me not to labor under the staggering load of constantly nurtured hurts.*
>
> *With strength from you, I will be able to give the past its proper role in my life—a helpful instructor. To do that, I need your presence and your grace.*
>
> *In the name of the One who never allowed past hurts to bankrupt his days, Amen.*

Disposing of Illusions

But Jesus did not commit himself unto them, because he knew all men, and needed not that any should testify of man: for he knew what was in man. (John 2:24-25)

Then said Jesus to those Jews which believed on him, If ye continue in my word, then are ye my disciples indeed; and ye shall know the truth, and the truth shall make you free. (John 8:31-32)

I don't remember ever thinking that with a little help from God, I was going to change the world. When I "surrendered to preach," I didn't dream about taking the denomination by storm or about becoming a boy wonder and heir apparent to the leading pulpiteer of the day. (And I always will be grateful that I never tried to imitate the popular evangelist of the time.) I remember saying with youthful idealism that I knew I would never make a lot of money (my only truly prophetic utterance), but that I liked people and wanted to help them. And I felt deeply that God had called me to preach. Later, I would broaden my concept; God had called me to minister. In some ways, I had my feet squarely on the ground.

But I had my illusions. A whole bunch of them. Subconsciously, I realize now, I felt that the acceptance for which I longed would be given. Surely God's people would take a preacher to their hearts. Too, I thought that a preacher would have sort of an inside track with God—protection, deeper fellowship, even a kind of favoritism. And churches certainly were filled with people of deep piety, warmth, openness, and a sweet spirit. I had other illusions about myself, God, the church, ministry—many of which have been laid to rest, one by one.

I am finding that more and more, I am becoming engaged in a process that is leading to a healthier way of living for me. The more I rid myself of illusions and learn to live with people and things as they are, the more I experience the abundant life of which Jesus spoke and which he brings. Jesus had no illusions, for he knew himself. He knew what was in people, what made them tick. He saw things as they were.

I still have my illusions. Some of them are slow in taking their leave. Hopefully, I am learning to call them by their proper names and am getting rid of some of them: the illusion that I can control the people and factors in my living; the naive assumption that adults in age are adults inside; the premise that I must come up with answers to all the religious, spiritual, and theological questions asked me; the notion that I can evade responsibility for myself by leaving everything to God. These and others are being replaced with realities that sometimes are harsh but which allow me to live in such a way that I no longer kid myself about some things. Most of us have a tendency to hang on to our illusions. We are comfortable with them. They help us to escape—at least temporarily—from painful, demanding reality. We say that things will work out somehow without our making maximum effort (as though things work at all). Success is out there somewhere, always tomorrow, and just over the hill. (This is what a friend of mine calls a distorted belief in miracles, a dependence on magic.) We contend that the most important thing is to be well-liked, at any cost; so we forfeit personhood. We believe, deep down, that money means Easy Street and happiness, that things—enough of them—bring contentment and peace. Many of us function by the principle that the end justifies the means. And some of us go on insisting that security comes from outside instead of from a sound center in ourselves.

We follow Christ in authentic living when we work at removing our illusions, and when we begin to deal with people and things as they are.

Lord, it is so easy to form illusions about ourselves, other people, the flow of life. And it is extremely difficult to get rid of them once we allow them to become set in our thinking. Yet, no matter how painful the leave-taking, I have a profound sense of freedom when one of my illusions is wrenched from its entrenched position in my life view. Thank you for helping me to confront truths about myself, others, and life. I really do want to see things as they are so that I can live life as you intended.

I will go on needing the courage, strength, and support that you alone can give for getting rid of illusions. Give me the gift of your presence as I continue to work on— and at—the life you have given me.

In the name of the One who knew the truth and lived it, Amen.

Acting on Impulse

And there came a leper to him, beseeching him, and kneeling down to him, and saying unto him, If thou wilt,

*thou canst make me clean. And Jesus, moved with com-
passion, put forth his hand, and touched him, and saith
unto him, I will; be thou clean. (Mark 1:40-41)*

*A certain man lame from his mother's womb was carried,
whom they laid daily at the gate of the temple which is
called Beautiful, to ask alms of them that entered into the
temple; who, seeing Peter and John about to go into the
temple asked an alms. And Peter, fastening his eyes
upon him with John, said, Look on us. And he gave
heed unto them, expecting to receive something of
them. Then Peter said, Silver and gold have I none; but
such as I have give I thee: In the name of Jesus Christ of
Nazareth rise up and walk. (Acts 3:2-6)*

He was old. He was unkempt, unwashed, and either sick or
hung over. He was sitting alone in a booth in a crowded eating
place in Norfolk, Virginia. A large number of us were standing near
the entrance, waiting for seated customers to finish their breakfasts
so that we could eat hurriedly and get to the morning session of the
Southern Baptist Convention. A waitress moved to the booth and
spoke to the old man, who then rose shakily and followed her as
she took his cup of coffee and a brown paper bag back to a storage
area. Four of us moved to sit down in the vacated booth. As we settled in and prepared to order breakfast, I felt the impulse to go back
to check on the old man—to see if he needed food, to make sure
that he was not sick, to do what I could to ensure that he was taken
care of in proper fashion.

On the heels of my first impulse came a second thought: "You
idiot! All these people are going to label your act as a grandstand
play if you go back there. Let the waitress handle it. You had better
stay where you are. Besides, you don't have much time before the
session starts." So I remained seated, eventually ate my meal, and
left.

Many times since those moments several years ago, I have
wished fervently that I had acted on my first impulse, the good one,
for I know that I have missed a moment that will not come again. In
the past, I had acted on impulse. I had said and done some things
on the spur of the moment when the better part of wisdom would

have been to stop and to think, to go slowly and carefully. Why had I hesitated to act on the impulse to do something good, something human in the highest sense of that word? Why do I sometimes still fail to act on a positive impulse, what is for me a rare flash of intuition?

We have those moments when we feel the strong urge to do some small act of good—to write a note, call, make a brief visit, give a gift, or compliment someone deserving. Often, if we fail to act quickly, the impulse fades and dies, and something fine and perhaps needed goes undone.

Lord, give me the courage, the wisdom, the kindness, and the true humanness you intend for me to have. Enable me to act on those urges to good that somehow I feel come from you. Let me have the necessary discipline and self-control to check impulses that are negative and destructive. Help me to act on your promptings to do that which is redemptive.

In the name of him who responded to human need without self-consciousness and with a great deal of compassion, Amen.

Creative Conflict

I beseech Euodias, and beseech Syntyche, that they be of the same mind in the Lord. And I entreat thee also, true yoke-fellow, help those women which laboured with me in the gospel. (Philippians 4:2-3a)

And the contention was so sharp between them, that they departed asunder one from the other: and so Barnabas took Mark, and sailed unto Cyprus; and Paul chose Silas, and departed, being recommended by the brethren unto the grace of God. (Acts 15:39-40)

For too long, my approach to interpersonal relationships in my various roles as staff member, pastor, husband, and employee has been to avoid conflict, usually at whatever cost this sidestepping has demanded. Only fairly recently have I begun to explore the idea that conflict can be creative. I am convinced—by experience and observation—that conflict is an inevitable reality with which we will be called on to deal repeatedly. It can be destructive, depreciating—or it can be a means of growth toward maturity.

Positively, conflict can get us in touch with our strengths. It can cause us to tap reserves of experience, education, and spiritual strength of which we had been unaware. Negatively, conflict can reveal our weaknesses. It can surface tendencies to allow the child in us to be hooked. It can cause sensitive, unresolved areas to become defined. It can bring into sharp focus needs to control, to be approved, to prove worth and competence. Conflict can be a valuable arena of learning about ourselves.

Conflict can let us see other people in a new light, if we are sensitive and aware. The person who shows through in conflict, with strengths and weaknesses, tendencies and needs, is the person to whom I must attempt to relate. When a person reveals where he or she really lives, then I have a chance to meet that person there in genuine openness.

Conflict can cause us to review repeatedly our positions, our arguments, in light of motive and logic to determine whether we act from feeling alone or from reason based on evidence. And the tension of difference can allow us to see merit in others' views.

Aside from an extremely small chip on the shoulder every great now and then (an unbiased view, of course), I have not gone looking for conflict. I do not plan to do so in the future. I have an idea that enough will occur in the normal flow of things. But neither do I intend to go on avoiding conflict at all costs. I hope to use it creatively—with the help of One who knew plenty of it while he was one of us and who never allowed it to be a negative experience.

This One who was—and is—well acquainted with conflict can use conflict positively. He can salvage something out of it. Long ago, in the church's beginning years, conflict arose between Paul and Barnabas. They parted company. In so doing, they formed two missionary teams which went out from Antioch. Instead of the one team that formerly labored, two went out to do the exacting work of sharing the good news. We are not told of Barnabas and Mark's work. We know something about Paul and Silas' labors. God has a way of using what comes, what he has to work with—even conflict.

Conflict is not to be invited. But when the unwelcome intruder shatters our peace, we have an opportunity to use it instead of being victimized by it.

Lord, I don't like conflict. I don't like the mixture of emotions stirred by a situation of tense confrontation — anger, anxiety, and sometimes fear. Often, my first reaction is to withdraw. But, then, when I do withdraw, I often feel anger at myself for not standing my ground and at least demanding a hearing for what I feel deeply. Help me never to go looking for conflict or to cause it by carelessness or violating another's freedom or rights. But enable me to work through conflict so that I learn lessons that will nudge me a little nearer to maturity as a person.

In the name of him who spent a great deal of his time dealing with conflict and who dealt with it in exemplary maturity, Amen.

Dealing with Disappointment

Without counsel purposes are disappointed: but in the multitude of counsellors they are established. (Proverbs 15:22)

O my God, my soul is cast down within me: therefore will I remember thee. (Psalm 42:6a)

It was what seemed to be an exciting, challenging opportunity. It was something in which I was interested intensely, and it promised multiple rewards, one of which was personal fulfillment. I found myself desperately wanting the chance. Then the word came: Someone else would get the job for which I had been considered. All my life, I had heard that God closes doors now and then. Nobody ever told me that, sometimes, he slams them in your face.

I experienced the bitter, lingering taste of disappointment. It was not the first time that I had been disappointed, and it would not be the last time I would know the feeling. In the future, I will face it again. But that one really hurt. The emotions came and were strong. I felt anger—at God, who wasn't helping; at people—who could give what I wanted and did not do so; at myself—for not being able to control factors vitally affecting my life and the lives of those people for whom I am responsible. I felt grief over loss of opportunity and possible achievement beyond where I was at the time. I had to deal with anxiety at the uncertainty of getting a second chance or an opportunity approaching the one so cruelly snatched from me. And I knew the ugly face of fear—fear of failure in a success-oriented society.

To look in stunned disbelief at the shattered pieces of a dream that all the theology in the world could not put back together again was not pleasant. I discovered that to stir the ashes of what once had been blazing hope is futile and frustrating. And the shout, "Why?"—no matter how loud and how sustained—was honored by silence. Again and again, I was thrown back on myself—and drawn to a few caring persons who shared.

What can I do in the cruel face of disappointment—in myself, other people, and the way things are? One response is to give in to the urge to do nothing, to become passive, stoic, and inert. It would be easy to see myself as put upon by the whole universe. I could do enough to get by and halt the costly pursuit of high personal goals.

A second response to disappointment is to adopt a "whatever will be, will be" attitude—or to use the convenient out of God's unbending will. This is to give in to the idea that my script already has been written and that I can do little or nothing to alter it. Thus, I become a perennial victim, an eternal pessimist.

A third response, an outgrowth of either or both of the first two, is to indulge in an ongoing game of "if only" and to plod on without hope. I can spend a great deal of my time looking back and lamenting: "If only I had gotten a break." I can look at people around me and reflect wistfully: "If only I had their tools, or influential friends, or chances."

A fourth response to disappointment is the one that I am convinced moves me on toward maturity. I can explore new avenues of opportunity with a dogged persistence that does not accept defeat until the final whistle blows. I can stand up to life and say: "I may go down, but I aim to make the fight as interesting as I can."

Disappointments come to all of us. They can be beginnings of the end, or they can be new beginnings.

Lord, disappointments seem to come at a fast pace for me. People sometimes don't turn out to be what I thought they were, or perhaps what I wanted them to be. I don't always function up to the level of inner standards by which I measure myself. Often, things don't go as I planned. And I find myself feeling down. In such moments, remind me that I probably disappoint people around me with some regularity. Help me to accept disappointments as a momentary experience from which I can learn — and from which I must turn in order to identify and examine options that are available to me.

I realize that I must have disappointed you countless times, yet you continue to work with me. Thank you for staying with me and not allowing my disappointing you to affect the way you relate to me.

In the name of the One who knew plenty of disappointments in his journey here, Amen.

Response to Despair

Why standest thou afar off, O Lord? Why hidest thou thyself in times of trouble? (Psalm 10:1)

How long wilt thou forget me, O Lord? for ever? How long wilt thou hide thy face from me? How long shall I take counsel in my soul, having sorrow in my heart daily? How long shall mine enemy be exalted over me? (Psalm 13:1-2)

Will the Lord cast off for ever? And will he be favourable no more? Is his mercy clean gone for ever? (Psalm 77:7-8a)

O Lord my God, in thee do I put my trust: save me from all them that persecute me, and deliver me: lest he tear my soul like a lion, rending it in pieces, while there is none to deliver. (Psalm 7:1-2)

It came as a new experience for me. It caught me completely off-guard and ill-prepared. I had known that life includes its valleys of deep shadows. I had preached that fact on more than one occasion. I had sat with people who were in their dark valleys, thinking that I knew a little something of what they felt, trying to offer some support. After all, I had experienced threat, stark and ugly. I had known grief, piercing and lingering. I had met disappointment, crushing and shattering. I had encountered failure, shaming and demeaning. But in all these experiences, I could see shafts of light up ahead, where eventually I would emerge from gloom into sunlight and open terrain and where I could get my bearings again as I continued my pilgrimage. Then I reached the valley of despair, and I found it to be long and deep, dark and lonely. Other people were there, in the shadows, but each person struggled alone.

Intense pressure was brought to bear on me and my family by individuals who were determined to bring me to my knees personally and professionally. And I found that the valley of the shadow of despair was more like a deep ravine whose sides were towering and sheer. I tried to climb those walls, to no avail. I tried running, only to drop in exhaustion. I tried sitting and waiting to be found, but the people who passed by felt threatened, could not help, or did not care.

What does a person do when his prayers meet with silence? When no light breaks through the gloom? When hope fades swiftly and joy becomes a bad joke? He can indulge in self-pity, express anger at God, get down on himself, blame other people—all of which I did. Or, he can get up and walk on in the shadows, holding stubbornly to the trust that the One who stands at the heart of the universe is loving, confessing, "Lord, I believe," asking, "Help my unbelief." One of the most difficult things I have done was to walk on in darkness, where no light at all broke through and the place of emerging could not be seen.

In my seemingly interminable valley, I literally learned to concentrate on the next step, on the immediate stretch of my way. I learned to take responsibility for my own life. I learned to do the best that I knew to do, one day at a time. When I decided, in stubborn anger, that I was going to stay on my feet, I began to emerge from despair. If my enemies came against me, as they came against the psalmists, I would meet them standing up, and I would give a good account of myself. I might not win; if I didn't, I was determined to lose with courage.

I don't know what lies ahead in my journey. Perhaps more treks through despair. But I aim to remain upright and moving, for I have discovered that on the far side of despair can lie inner strength, renewed faith in a God who goes with us in his silent way, and a needed sensitivity to despairing people.

Lord, even now, on the far side of despair and looking back at the receding valley, a shiver flashes through me. It wasn't a pleasant experience, and I can't thank you for it. I can thank you for the awareness that you were there, in the shadows, moving silently. I can express my gratitude that now I can identify to some degree with despairing people. Help me to be sensitive to the sounds and gestures of despondent people who are enduring a long night's journey toward an uncertain sunrise.

In the name of him who has infinite compassion for despairing people, Amen.

What Follows Failure?

And about the space of one hour after another confidently affirmed, saying, Of a truth this fellow also was with him: for he is a Galilean. And Peter said, Man, I know not what thou sayest. And immediately, while he yet spake, the cock crew. And the Lord turned, and looked upon Peter. And Peter remembered the word of the Lord, how he had said unto him, Before the cock crow, thou shalt deny me thrice. And Peter went out, and wept bitterly. (Luke 22:59-62)

One of the things that many of us fear most is failure. For as long as I can remember, it has been one of my deepest, most persistent fears. It is one thing to know intellectually that we all fail at some point in our journeys. It is something else entirely to accept it as fact for us and to deal with it emotionally.

I had worked long and hard on my doctoral thesis. I had set a goal for submitting it, taking my oral examination, and graduating. As my self-imposed deadline neared, I pushed myself. I rushed some actions to which I should have given more time. I was not as careful as I should have been. The thesis was turned back to me. I had made numerous mechanical errors which needed to be corrected. I would have to clean up my work and resubmit it.

Other students before me had not gotten their theses through on the first try. I had been aware of that fact and of the possibility that I might not make it on the first submission. Still, my failure came as a severe jolt. I had labored intensely; I had had a goal that seemed reasonable; I was emotionally "up" for the oral exam and the defense of my thesis. Then came the pin applied to my balloon and the swift deflation of my hope.

Somewhere in my graduate-school experience I had heard, almost in passing, what had struck me as wise counsel. Someone had failed on his first thesis submission. He had said that his salvation from failure had been to go to the library on the morning after his shattering experience and to plunge back into the work of correcting his errors. The day after my dream had exploded, I went about my secular job during the morning. I returned to my room, cleaned up, ate lunch, collected my defective thesis, and planted myself in a library carrel. To borrow a phrase from sports, I "got after it."

The effort was not easy. On that first day of my trek toward recovery from failure, a graduate-school "brother" passed my carrel and offered the unsolicited opinion: "It's a little late for that now. You should have thought of it earlier." To this day, I regret that I did not follow through on the urge to punch him in the nose. Instead, I went on working.

I did what I knew to do. Eventually, I made it. And I learned that the only valid response to failure is to collect all the pieces you can find of a project, a dream, an ambition, and to get back to work on the alternative that is available to you.

Simon Peter failed. He had made a lofty pronouncement of his loyalty to Christ. When the chips were down, he failed. He wept as he gazed into the mocking face of failure. But to his everlasting credit, he didn't give up on Christ—or on himself. He stayed with it, and because he did Christ was able to make him marvelously useful in the Christian movement.

John Mark failed. At least, one possibility is that he turned back in the face of a demanding missionary task. He must have stayed with it, because later Paul wrote that Mark was "profitable for the ministry."

Jesus was not always successful with every person. He could do no mighty works in Nazareth because of the people's unbelief, and he failed to win the rich young ruler. But Jesus went on to the next town, the next person. He went on with his work.

Failure is not the end, unless we make it so. Almost always, it is a jarring experience that may stop us in our tracks—momentarily. But failure can become a rich mine of learning—about ourselves and other people. Failure at one endeavor may free us to look at other options. It may move us to assess where we are and where we want to be. We might dig deeper into the spiritual reserves that we have built up in character—or to find that these are not available but are vital to our living. Failure can move us closer to those few people whom we can trust and who care—and to Jesus who accepted those who had failed and gave them a new beginning.

When we fail, we can pick ourselves up and get back into the race. Or, we can drop out as those who are afraid to try again and who are resigned to failure. To fail doesn't necessarily mean to become a failure. We can go on with renewed determination. We become failures when we quit.

What follows failure? Resignation, or renewed effort?

Lord, I live in a society where success defined in secular terms is a god at whose temple multitudes worship. The rallying cry of my time is "Win!"—no matter what, no matter how. My society loves winners and rewards them lavishly. Losers are the lowest caste in America's well-defined system, outcasts to be ignored or removed from the landscape.

But Lord, so many losers look longingly and anxiously for a place to begin again, for an opportunity to experience some measure of self-fulfillment, for some degree of self-worth. Thank you that a minority of sensitive, caring people reach out to the outcasts of my time and place. Help me to be more of an encourager, an enabler, a supportive friend to persons struggling to escape an enslaving stigma.

And when I lose, remind me forcefully that I only be-

*come a loser when I refuse to get up—with your help—
and to go on.*

*In the name of the One who reached out to the losers
of his day with a love that convinced them they were
somebodies instead of nobodies, Amen.*

Facing My Fears

*And he said unto them, Why are ye so fearful? how is it
that ye have no faith? (Mark 4:40)*

*Let not your heart be troubled, neither let it be afraid.
(John 14:27b)*

*For ye have not received the spirit of bondage again to
fear; but ye have received the Spirit of adoption, where-
by we cry, Abba, Father. (Romans 8:15)*

*For God hath not given us the spirit of fear; but of power,
and of love, and of a sound mind. (2 Timothy 1:7)*

*There is no fear in love; but perfect love casteth out fear:
because fear hath torment. He that feareth is not made
perfect in love. (1 John 4:18)*

Somewhere in my growing-up years, the idea was impressed on
me and remained strong for a long time. Boys—and men—were
not to be afraid. Fear was not to be included in a secure, courageous, mature male's vocabulary. One of my goals became to
move to the point where I was not afraid of anything or anybody. I
experienced perpetual struggle, for I discovered that deep down,
nagging fears surfaced periodically. I admired those persons who
seemed to know no fear, and I was frustrated with my inability to
banish fear from myself.

It came as a startling insight from a caring, sensitive person that
all people fear something or many things. When I was helped to see
this truth, I also was helped to begin to deal with my fears. I began
to see that to experience fear is not shameful or degrading. Fear is

another of our emotions that can be useful or destructive. A mark of wisdom is to know whom or what to fear and then to move to take care of ourselves, the persons nearest to us, and other people who are threatened with harm.

All of us have nagging fears, shadowy feelings deep down that tear at our insides, drain our emotional energy, and reduce our effectiveness as persons. We add to their power to diminish us by allowing them to remain nameless and faceless. One mark of a developing maturity is the courage to look our fears "right in the eyes," to call them by their proper names, and to begin to examine them.

What do we fear? For several years, I have tried to label my fears honestly. I haven't been successful as often as I would like, but I have found that my fears lose a lot of their strength when I bring them into the light. One fear that I carried for years was the fear of failure. If I failed, I reasoned, people would not like or accept me; I had to achieve. I remember what I told my mother as I prepared for the unknown, somewhat threatening world of college. In essence, I told her that I might not make it in college, but I wanted her to know that if I failed, I would have tried my best. I was preparing her—and myself—for the possibility of failure. All along my way, I have been dogged by the fear of failure. But now, when this fear comes barging into consciousness, I can deal with it. I know its name and its face. I know that failure, even in a success-oriented society, does not have to be terminal and is not confined to a few people. I know what some of my strengths are, and I am aware that I need not limit my alternatives. Fear of failure may come and go in my experience. I refuse to give it permanent residency.

Other fears crop up now and then: the fear of my being viewed by other people as incompetent or, at best, barely adequate; the fear of serious illness and of slowly declining health; the fear of aging; the fear of difficulty; the fear of death. I have heard these fears expressed. Sometimes, I have seen evidences of them when people would not, or could not, put names to them.

The first step in dealing with our fears is to face them squarely and to label them correctly. Then, we can express these to a competent, caring, sensitive person. Fears continue to lose their power to immobilize life when they are verbalized. Fears are defused further when we realize that other people share the same or similar fears. Most of all, fears can be neutralized and overcome by a strong faith in God who is present to share in all our experiences. Too, fears diminish when we realize that we are loved supremely. When life rests on the grace of God expressed in Jesus the Christ, then that life never will be defeated by the circumstances of life or by death. For, as Paul stated so well in Romans 8, Christians will encounter nothing that "shall be able to separate us from the love of God, which is in Christ Jesus our Lord" (Rom. 8:39).

Long ago, in the face of his fears the psalmist made his marvelous, timeless statement of faith: "The Lord is my light and my salvation; whom shall I fear? The Lord is the strength of my life; of whom shall I be afraid?" (Ps. 27:1). With that kind of courageous faith, we can face our fears.

> *Lord, no matter how much Scripture encourages us not to be afraid, we struggle with our fears. Some of us struggle in secret so that others will not see that we are afraid. Some of us struggle silently because we do not know understanding people to whom we can go to express what we feel. We walk through our valleys of deep darkness and we do fear what can happen to us. In a faith that overcomes fear, help us to reaffirm that you alone can keep our fears from immobilizing us—that only you can help us to work through our fears to courage, peace, and hope.*
>
> *I identify strongly with that marvelous psalmist who wrote: "What time I am afraid, I will trust in thee." Thank you for those inspired words of an honest individual. I probably never will be fearless, but help me to hold on to my trust in you.*
>
> *In the name of him who never gave in to fear but understands ours, Amen.*

The Shape of Hope

Why art thou cast down, O my soul? And why art thou disquieted in me? Hope thou in God: for I shall yet praise him for the help of his countenance. (Psalm 42:5)

Abraham . . . who against hope believed in hope. (Romans 4:16b,18)

My days are swifter than a weaver's shuttle, and are spent without hope. (Job 7:6)

A few years ago, during one stretch of my journey as a person, I had been on a seemingly endless roller coaster ride. I climbed slowly to high peaks of vibrant hope, only to plunge with breathtaking speed to deep dips of hopelessness. I knew what "hoping against hope" meant—looking for a better day despite all the indications of continuing storm and threat. I learned to discipline elation so that I did not "get my hopes up" too high. If I didn't hope intensely, the fall wouldn't be quite so long. The jolt on hitting the ground again wouldn't be quite so jarring.

Hope had become a jokester that I could no longer trust—except when hope came in the shape of caring persons. I discovered that the only genuine hope I received was in the form of sensitive, open, warmly human people. Not religious people bent on doing their Christian duty whether or not they were welcome. Not answer people who attempted to give simple answers to complicated problems. Not necessarily people of power and influence who could get for me what I wanted. But people who came to stand where I stood and by doing so to say wordlessly: "We care."

I realized that people of quality are the real miracles still occurring—people who embody hope because they dare to share other people's pain and agony. They run the real risk involved in being helping persons. They are the people who incarnate hope.

My discovery changed me drastically—and positively. It caused me to become more empathetic with my brothers, some of whom I formerly would not have given the time of day. Our personalities and theologies clashed. Our approaches and positions in life differed. But I was helped to see those as trivial and meaningless items. What matters is that we all are on a tough, exacting pilgrimage together. Now, I find myself wanting intensely to embody hope for at least a few other people. One of my priorities is to give hope. If I cannot give people all the help they need, then I can stand where they stand as one person who is concerned.

Hope, when it comes again to me, will come in the shape of a caring person. For I have found that hope wears a human face. God gives hope, not out of the blue I am convinced—at least, not to me. God gives hope through people whom he sends into the center of others' storms.

Lord, I know the theological definition of hope: confidence which comes from you, based on who you are and what you can do. I have done a lot of wishful thinking that has masqueraded as hope. I have known luminous moments when hope lighted my steps. And I have experienced moments when hope flickered and almost died. Again and again, I come back to a stubborn trust that you are faithful in your care for those who are open to you.

Thank you for all those persons who have incarnated hope for me. Some have cared, not because I was worthy, but because I was there. Help me to put a human face on hope for others I meet.

In the name of the One who brought—and brings—the only real hope people have, Amen.

On Being Angry

And when he had looked round about on them with anger, being grieved for the hardness of their hearts, he saith unto the man, Stretch forth thine hand. And he stretched it out: and his hand was restored whole as the other. (Mark 3:5)

And the Jews' passover was at hand, and Jesus went up to Jerusalem, and found in the temple those that sold oxen and sheep and doves, and the changers of money sitting: and when he had made a scourge of small cords, he drove them all out of the temple, and the sheep, and the oxen; and poured out the changers' money, and overthrew the tables; and said unto them that sold doves, Take these things hence; make not my Father's house an house of merchandise. (John 2:13-16)

When I heard the phrase used in the caring group of which I was a part, I knew immediately that it applied to me. I was put in touch with something going on in me for which I had had no label. For the first time, I was helped to understand some of my feelings and actions that sometimes defied my attempts to examine and explain them, some of my words and acts that sometimes hurt the people closest to me.

"Free-floating anger" is the phrase. I was introduced to the fact that my anger at other things and other people—and myself—can be vented on my wife, my children, the "Sunday driver" in the next lane (or creeping along ahead of me), a congregation "told off" in the name of the Lord, or an inanimate object with the ill fortune of getting in my way.

I am convinced that I have tried to minister—and still relate to and encounter—a large number of people unaware of their free-floating anger, anger looking for an unwary, unsuspecting victim. Some individuals are angry at God for letting them down, not listening to them, or not giving a desired blessing. But they can't—or don't dare—admit it. Some people are angry at other persons for not anticipating their needs and moving to meet them. Some of us are angry at people on whom we cannot vent our anger because of their positions of influence or their power over us. Many of us are angry at ourselves for our failure to meet our own inner standards, for not making it to the top of the heap, for not being one of the beautiful people. Such anger often is directed toward anyone or anything that is convenient, targets for a misplaced rage.

Jesus felt and expressed anger—not righteous indignation, I am convinced, but anger. However, he was angry at the right people and circumstances, for the right reasons, at the right times, and in the right ways. His anger was channeled, controlled, creative. He made good use of a valuable emotion by unleashing it redemptively.

Most of us waste a great deal of our anger. We don't call it by the correct name. We don't direct it toward the right objects or persons. We suppress it instead of dealing with it. Too often, we victimize each other with our anger.

To be angry and to acknowledge and deal with our anger is all right. To feel it, to fail to label it properly, and to do violence to the personalities of unsuspecting—and many times innocent—persons-made-objects is not all right. Anger is a God-given emotion. We must work to use it constructively, not destructively.

Lord, go on challenging me to put away childish temper tantrums and nurtured rage. Help me to identify my anger and its true sources and objects. Save me from incorrect, useless, destructive anger. But enable me constructively to be angry at those things in my world that should draw my anger: greed that sacrifices persons for money; prejudice that reduces people to objects, or to nothing; intolerance that will not allow others their rightful freedom to be and to do; poverty and hunger that still ravage so many lives in "the land of plenty" and around my world. Help me to be so angry at destructive forces and people that I will attempt to do something corrective, redemptive. Cause my anger to move me to take some step, no matter how small, to right the wrong and to alleviate the suffering and injustice that I encounter.

In the name of him who showed us the right way to use anger, Amen.

Spectacular Religion

Then the devil taketh him up into the holy city, and setteth him on a pinnacle of the temple, and saith unto him, If thou be the Son of God, cast thyself down: for it is written, He shall give his angels charge concerning thee: and in their hands they shall bear thee up, lest at any time thou dash thy foot against a stone. Jesus said unto him, It is written again, Thou shalt not tempt the Lord thy God. (Matthew 4:5-7)

It came in the mail several times while I was a pastor—a flyer advertising the wares of an evangelistic team. A member of the singing team did a remarkable imitation. The major attractions were two poodles who performed a wide variety of tricks. They attracted children who had to be brought by parents, thus ensuring a large crowd. I thought of a friend of mine who, a number of years ago, after hearing what is still one of today's most popular religious singing teams, whispered to me: "All we need now is a tiger." Seeing my blank expression and knowing that he had lost me, he said: "To have a first-rate circus in this sanctuary, all we need is a tiger to go with that group."

The trend toward spectacular entertainment as a setting for proclaiming the good news reminds me of something that Jesus refused to do as he prepared to begin his public ministry. One alternative which presented itself to him concerning gaining a hearing, response from the people, and the support of the masses, was to "do his act." He could throw himself off the pinnacle of the Temple and come out miraculously unhurt, without a scratch. That would attract plenty of attention and draw quite a crowd of followers. But Jesus discarded that alternative as unacceptable; nobody presumes on God. Too, a crowd attracted by the spectacular would expect more and more of the same—or better. What do you do to follow up a miracle—or a dog act? Jesus refused to give a sign to the religious leaders who requested that he do so to authenticate his messiahship to them. He was not interested in gaining giddy spectators to a religious sideshow.

What Jesus did, as I view him in the Gospels, was to announce clearly and uncompromisingly the good news as gift and demand. He issued the call, "Follow me!" He was not concerned that people be entertained. He was concerned that they be enlightened and challenged, brought to decision about him, and called into his difficult way—not as a second act of a show, but in answer to a primary summons to repentance and redemptive living. Spectacular religion is shallow and misleading. Responsible discipleship is a daily answering to the Lord of life. There is a rather significant difference in the two.

Lord, I sometimes wonder if you would not have a more difficult time gaining a hearing if you came physically into my society than you did nearly two thousand years ago. I wonder this not just because of the general callousness and indifference that is so prevalent in my society, but because we are so accustomed to being entertained. We demand performances that tingle nerve ends that have been made insensitive by an insatiable appetite for the exciting, the new, the unusual. I wonder if your clear, simple call would be heard above the roar and din of a society threatened by silence, simplicity, and reflective thought. And after your first miracle-with-a-message, I wonder if the message would be heard above the demand for more and better miracles. In a society which pays people millions of dollars to entertain, your act would be in demand. But I have an idea that your message would not be highly marketable.

Help me to know the difference between entertainment and worship, performance and ministry, excitement and inspiration. Enable me to insist on and maintain that difference.

In the name of him who worshiped, ministered, and inspired but never performed or entertained in order to manipulate people, Amen.

3

"The Church, . . . His Body"
(Ephesians 1:22-23)

Much of my life to this point has been spent in local churches. For fourteen-plus years, I have been pastor of or have served on the staffs of four churches. I have been a member of and active in three others. In each of these seven churches, I have had positive and negative experiences that have contributed to my growth as a person and as a Christian. Some of these experiences have altered the direction of my journey and have helped me to arrive at the present point or teachable moment.

Everything that has happened to me in local churches has sparked and reinforced a deep conviction: An ongoing miracle that is taking place in our day is what the Lord of the church is able to accomplish through his Body and through each local expression of that Body. Local churches are made up of diverse people—people who differ widely in personality, motivation, commitment, levels of maturity. Yet, Christ goes on working through local churches to continue his ministry to people.

My debt to the churches is beyond paying. Largely through my foundational church, I was led to commit my life to Christ. A number of people had input into that decision. Then, that local church had influence on my choice to enter a church-related vocation. The others contributed to my being trained and equipped for ministry—and to my being forced to rid myself of numerous naive ideas and to work on myself and my approach to ministry.

Some of the people in the churches where I worshiped and worked always will retain a special place in my memory. They gave of themselves in love and concern; in so doing, they reinforced my hope for the church.

From the First Day

I thank my God upon every remembrance of you, always in every prayer of mine for you all making request

*with joy, for your fellowship in the gospel from the first
day until now. (Philippians 1:3-5)*

*Now ye Philippians know also, that in the beginning of
the gospel, when I departed from Macedonia, no church
communicated with me as concerning giving and receiving, but ye only. (Philippians 4:15)*

I sometimes stop to think of my heritage, the background or
foundation of what I am and where I am in my journey as a person
and as a Christian. I acknowledge repeatedly my debt to two
churches who played crucial roles in my early direction and development in life.

The First Baptist Church of Lumberton, Mississippi is not, and
never has been, large numerically. But it has been a strong church
because of good leadership and committed followers. During my
developing years, much of my time was spent in activities of that
fellowship. I learned a lot, much more than I realized for quite a
while. I now know that some of the theology to which I was exposed was not always the soundest, but I was exposed to the ba-
sics. I learned more from the lives of people who gave their time to
teach me, to plan and conduct activities for my enjoyment and my
benefit, and to challenge me.

Most of all, I received the genuine care of a number of people
who made it clear that a skinny little kid mattered. He was worth
their efforts. When I made my commitment to the pastoral ministry,
their support and encouragement was incredible—from the first
day. I look back and wince at the "preaching" to which they were
subjected as I held forth periodically in an attempt to develop in my
role. Not one time did they fail to respond with encouraging compli-
ments. All along the way in those early, fledgling years, they gave
the unhesitating support that I needed. No matter how poorly I
functioned, no one ever hinted that I was anything less than the
surefire successor to the day's outstanding pulpiteer. Those people
have my lasting gratitude. Some of them are gone, but I remember
them warmly. Some are still there, no doubt encouraging and supporting others on their way.

A few miles west of my hometown is the small community of
Baxterville. I went to school with some people from that commu-

nity. I played baseball there on a number of occasions as a boy. My dad worked near there at two points during his working days. Twice during my long tenure as a seminary student, the Baxterville Baptist Church asked me to preach during interims between pastors. Both times, the invitations came at most opportune moments for me. My bank account was getting dangerously low, and I was concerned about meeting school expenses. Both times, the church paid me well—and probably overpaid me. More than money, they let me share the warmth of their fellowship. They offered friendship and encouragement. They gave me needed confidence in myself.

Two churches, with many differences, contributed significantly to my life in tangible ways. More importantly, they contributed priceless intangibles. They were made up of different kinds of people, some of whom made ongoing efforts to give of themselves with no thought of being repaid. I can't pay them for their gifts to me. I can, and do, thank them for their giving much to me and receiving little from me—from the first day until now.

Lord, now and then I remember some of the earlier stretches of my journey as a person, a Christian, a pastor-in-training. And I remember with gratitude. So many people have helped me along my way. Churches have played important roles in what progress I have made. I thank you for all of them, for each contribution they made. May my memories of persons and churches cause me to be sensitive to my opportunities to help beginning Christians and people in religious vocations. Help me to take the time and make the effort to offer the encouragement that some will need as they make their way.

In the name of the One who means for his church to be a fellowship of enablers and encouragers, Amen.

On Being the Church

Unto the church of God which is at Corinth, to them that are sanctified in Christ Jesus, called to be saints, with all

*that in every place call upon the name of Jesus Christ our
Lord, both theirs and ours. (1 Corinthians 1:2)*

*Now ye are the body of Christ, and members in particu-
lar. (1 Corinthians 12:27)*

The most beautiful church-building exterior that I have seen is in
Mobile, Alabama. The most beautiful interior of a church building
that I have examined is in Anniston, Alabama. The largest church
edifice that I have gazed at in awe is in New York City. The smallest
church auditorium that I have seen, I preached in. The warmest fellowship I have felt is that of a group of people meeting for worship
in an attractive, neat, unpretentious building in a rural community.
The last church has made the deepest, most lasting impression on
me.

I find myself—and hear other people—using the phrase "going to
church." Many of us have gone far beyond the time when we
should have explored seriously the creative concept of *being* the
church. My observation has been that those who know themselves
to be the church, gathered for worship or scattered for ministry, do
not need the newest—or the oldest and most hackneyed—
promotional gimmicks in order to involve them in the activities of
the company. Their concern is not so much their support of a *pro
gram* as it is their response to a Person who is not confined to
appointed times and places.

Many of us have gone on asking the wrong question, when we
ask at all. "Why don't you come (or come back) to church this Sunday?" must be replaced with a more basic, probing challenge:
"When are we going to begin to *be* the church?" All of our church-
going to this point seems to have worked little, if any, significant
change. But we cannot be the church in the various facets of our living without being in the process of personal change and helping to
effect change around us.

Some of the people who are the church meet in buildings on
Main Street, Fifty-Eighth Avenue, Hogan Road, or Route 3. But
when these people are scattered on other streets, avenues, roads,
and lanes, our society sees the church at work, at play, in ministry—not in a setting of stained glass, soft organ music, carefully
worded prayers, and robust hymns. The church is observed in ac-

tion in the swift, turbulent current of life's common affairs. We are the church there, or we are not really Christ's church at all. We are another organization competing for time and funds, but we are not the body of Christ extending his messianic ministry to his world.

The church scattered gives cups of cold water, helps to heal hurts, listens, and shares good news. People will come to the places where the church meets in worship when we who are the church meet them in life's give-and-take with real care.

> *Lord, remind me that I represent you no matter what I am doing or where I am. In a real sense, I am the church. I may be all the church that some will see and have contact with. Help me to represent you in a worthy manner. And may what I show of what being the church means, be a reason for people to be drawn to you and what you are doing. Bless all those people who know themselves to be your church dispersed in various areas of their society. When they meet, may they be equipped for ever increasing effectiveness in ministry. When they go their varied ways, may they have a real sense of mission.*
>
> *In the name of the One who gave himself for his church, Amen.*

The Church's First Task

And the Lord came, and stood, and called as at other times, Samuel, Samuel. Then Samuel answered, Speak; for thy servant heareth. (1 Samuel 3:10)

For too long a time, my approach to the subject of the church's primary tasks remained in a well-worn groove: The major work of the church—any church—was to share the good news of the Christ, to be engaged in ministry to the total person, to provide resources necessary for people to grow toward spiritual maturity. Then, I chanced to read Elizabeth O'Connor's fine little book, *Search for Silence*. She pointed to a prior task on which I had placed minor and sporadic emphasis. My emphases had been right, but something else had to come first before anything else was done.

As a student of theology, and then as a pastor, I had been exposed to the concept. But Elizabeth O'Connor placed it in proper perspective for me when she wrote that the church's primary task is to be attentive to God's Word. The first priority of any church is to listen while God speaks.

The idea makes sense to me. It has the ring of truth. Before we announce the good news and explore its implications for our lives, we must hear it clearly—all of it. Before we can minister to the totality of persons' lives, we must receive proper directives and be motivated to genuine care. Before we can nurture growing Christians, we must listen for the words of life that sustain. Before we speak or act, we first must listen for the Word from God, in whatever form and by whatever means it may come.

I have wondered why too often we do not listen for the sounds of God. Not many of us do, you know. Could we be afraid of what we will be forced to see about ourselves? Do we suspect, vaguely or strongly, that the Word may be one of demand, causing us discomfort and inconvenience—and perhaps costing more than we are willing to give? Perhaps the Word may command to a direction that we refuse to choose for ourselves or our church. Whatever the reason or reasons, too many of us don't listen often or well to the God whom we claim as Father.

We may have forgotten or neglected the one thing we must do as individuals and collectively as churches in order to become effective as people ministering in Christ's spirit. We well may need to say in total seriousness to the God who listens to us: "Speak, for your servants hear"—and then listen.

> *Lord, I have an idea that all too often, I and others of your people fail to pause long enough to hear what you are trying to say to us. We have our plans, dreams, programs, projects for our churches and for our personal lives. We have a tendency to try to work things out in our own wisdom, in our own strength. Help us to wait for your Word, as clearly as we can understand it—and to wait for the necessary power from you, just as Jesus had his disciples to wait before they started their work.*
>
> *In the name of the One who still speaks in a variety of ways to those who listen, Amen.*

On Being Ministry Oriented

Yea, and if I be offered upon the sacrifice and service of your faith, I joy, and rejoice with you all. (Philippians 2:17)

I know thy works, and charity, and service, and faith, and thy patience, and thy works; and the last to be more than the first. (Revelation 2:19)

My observation has been that many of the churches that I know about from firsthand experience are either meeting oriented or ministry oriented. Seldom, if ever, are they both. Some meet to eat, meet to discuss, meet to fight (religiously), meet to meet. Others have a minimum of meetings—and these are well planned, concise, productive—and a maximum of involvement in creative ministry. This observation has made me uncomfortable. It has produced an ongoing tension in me. I see so much meeting-for-the-slightest-reason. I long to be part of effective ministry.

Meetings are necessary. *Some* meetings are necessary. People must meet in order to plan, organize, project, and enjoy other people's company in a relaxed atmosphere of real fellowship. But the danger—and it is real and grave—is that meetings become ends instead of means. We can come to feel that meetings are acts of service which allow us to discharge a large measure of our obligation to Christ through his church. And we can fail to move beyond meeting to encounter people with their wide spectrum of needs. I have begun to wonder if perhaps some churches meet so much that most of the people's energy is spent in this area and none is left for the real work of the church. And I also have wondered if a preponderance of meetings can indicate that a church has turned its attention inward, on itself.

As a pastor, I wrestled with the idea of my churches' becoming more ministry oriented. The why of the effort to accent service was never difficult. By its nature, a church is a servant company. The how of implementing the change took a great deal of thought and work—and then sometimes no change occurred. But I am convinced that together, people can make creative change and can become a group of ministers to their community. Then they will

meet to explore new avenues of service and new ways to implement their servant role as Christ's people. But they will spend much
more of their time responding to genuine needs than coming together to talk.

> *Lord, remind me repeatedly that in my church, I am a*
> *minister among ministers. Help me to be prepared and*
> *willing to serve, not just inside the company, but wher-*
> *ever I meet needs. Enable me to be ministry oriented and*
> *thus to influence my church to move toward fulfilling its*
> *servant role.*
> *In the name of the One who saw himself as Suffering*
> *Servant and modeled the servant role for all of us,*
> *Amen.*

Incentive for Worship

> *And he came to Nazareth, where he had been brought*
> *up: and, as his custom was, he went into the synagogue*
> *on the sabbath day, and stood up for to read. (Luke*
> *4:16)*

I can't understand Christians who are casual about, or derelict in,
their participation in collective worship. I can understand why some
people would not be thrilled overmuch to hear me preach—or
some other preachers I have endured. I realize, from my years of
sitting in a pew, that some worship periods are weary exercises in
boredom. And I know that some folks so easily get crossed up in
their dealings with each other that they don't care to sit in the same
church auditorium together. At least, that's what any number of
church dropouts have told me. But for the life of me, I can't understand those individuals who claim to be related to Christ and whose
involvement in collective worship is seldom, sporadic, or nonexis-
tent—afterthoughts or footnotes to their living, if part of it at all.

One factor in my rethinking of the significance of collective worship is a brief phrase in Luke 4:16. Jesus had returned to Nazareth,
where he had grown up. Luke wrote: "And, as his custom was, he
went into the synagogue on the sabbath day." Jesus considered

gathering with God's people in a place designated for worship and on a day set aside for worship to be important. He sometimes led such worship periods. But not always, I am convinced. Sometimes he must have taken his place in the congregation, listening to Scripture being read as though hearing it for the first time, sharing moments of devotion with people wanting a word from God for the pressures of their living.

If I felt no need for the fellowship of other Christians or for a word of challenge, inspiration, or comfort from God or for more light for my living, I still would feel incentive to participate with some regularity in collective worship. I would want to discover, if at all possible, what Jesus found so meaningful and helpful in it. Anything he made it a habit to do must be right for me, offering something to help me along in my pilgrimage.

> *Lord, sometimes I don't feel like worshiping. I grow lazy and listless, or I feel down and just want to stay home rather than gather with your people for worship. And even when I do attend worship, I sometimes am not as attentive and prayerful as I should be. Help me to be reminded of the value of collective worship and to give more of myself to it.*
>
> *Thank you for deep worship experiences which were shared with others and which offered material for my living. A prayer, a song, a Scripture passage, a sermon, a phrase from a sermon—something in the process of worship usually speaks to me when I am open to your presence.*
>
> *Help me to work at contributing to an atmosphere in which others can worship "in spirit and in truth."*
>
> *In the name of the One for whom worship was a way of life, Amen.*

Motivation for Serious Study of Scripture

And when the tempter came to him, he said, If thou be the Son of God, command that these stones be made bread. But he answered and said, It is written, Man shall

*not live by bread alone, but by every word that proceed-
eth out of the mouth of God. (Matthew 4:3-4)*

One morning, during the preparation of a sermon for an onrush-
ing Sunday, I was writing about Jesus' familiarity with the Psalms
and his use of them during his ministry. I thought about his frequent, effective use of his Scriptures, the Old Testament. I was
reminded of something of which I have been convinced for a long
time: Jesus must have spent countless hours in prayerful study of
Scripture.

From earliest instruction in his home, from synagogue training,
from his own private study, he came to an amazing knowledge of,
and interpretation of, Scripture. Jesus did not just pick out of the air
words from Deuteronomy and Psalms during the temptations in the
wilderness; *he had lived with those words.* He made no spur of the
moment decision when he read from Isaiah in Nazareth; the Servant Songs had become the shape of his ministry. His quotation
from Exodus, used to counter the Sadducees' denial of resurrection, was an interpretation worked out long before that encounter.
His quotation of the opening words of Psalm 22 while he was dying
indicates, at least to me, that this was a psalm to which he had gone
again and again as he faced a mounting crisis, words to which he
held tightly as the light of life began to flicker and go out.

If Jesus lived with Scripture and found there substance for his living, then something just might be there for me if I am willing to
spend the time to dig it out, examine it, and store it away to be used
in the complexity of my living, in meeting a multiplicity of demands.
If Scripture was so valuable to Jesus and had something to do with
the quality of his life, then I would like to follow in his steps here. As
I move along through life, I am discovering that I need all the help
that I can get. I need all the spiritual material that I can gather for
my journey in order that I may live and not merely exist. The words
of life and *for* life can be—must be—light for my path.

*Lord, thank you for the marvelous treasury that you
have given to us in the Scriptures. Forgive me for sometimes taking the Bible for granted or for being indifferent
to it. Motivate me to read the Scriptures devotionally so*

*that I may gain valuable material for my living. Help me
to study the Bible analytically so that I may interpret it
correctly when I share its words.*

*In the name of him who is the center of the Scriptures
and who serves as the standard by whom they must be
understood, Amen.*

On Cutting the Unemployment Rate

*And he gave some, apostles; and some, prophets; and
some, evangelists; and some, pastors and teachers; for
the perfecting of the saints, for the work of the ministry,
for the edifying of the body of Christ. (Ephesians
4:11-12)*

"A community which allows unemployed members to exist within it will perish because of them. It will be well, therefore, if every
member receives a definite task to perform for the community, that
he may know in hours of doubt that he, too, is not useless and un-
usable."[1] Dietrich Bonhoeffer wrote these startling words in his
work, *Life Together.*

The words set me to thinking in a new direction. One of the
major concerns of our day is the high rate of unemployment; in
fact, some people feel that *any* unemployment is unacceptable. I
have deep feeling for the people who want to work and support
their families but who have no jobs available to them. I have trouble
with those individuals who can work but who find ever-new ways to
avoid being gainfully employed and who are content to live off
other people. But I really had not thought much about—or felt
for—persons within my Christian community who were jobless in
the work of ministry. The rate of unemployment in my church is
extremely high. Some simply do not want to work. But some have
no specific jobs to do because the church does not engage in the
exacting work of calling them to responsibility and encouraging
them to use their creativity.

The unemployed persons within a church comprise a tragedy of
immense proportions. They deprive themselves—or are de-

prived—of needed development, the stretching of their lives. They deprive their church of needed contributions to the company's ministry—or are not asked to add their strength of life to corporate service.

We can cut churches' unemployment rates. We must work to enlist useful people and to entrust them with jobs which allow self-expression and a sense of achievement. To fail to do so is to make the choice to become ineffectual as churches.

> *Lord, help me to be sensitive to those in my particular fellowship who are jobless but who have shining potential to minister. Enable me to see their gifts and to help them see and develop them. In order to be a minister among ministers, I will need to encourage, to support, to share. Only your grace can give me the proper motivation to take the time and to make the effort out of no other incentive than goodwill. Yet, I ask that you make me one small part of a church busy employing its members in meaningful work that has spiritual growth as a by-product.*
>
> *In the name of the One who called—and calls—every person into his work force, Amen.*

Note

1. Dietrich Bonhoeffer, *Life Together* (New York: Harper & Row, Publishers, Inc., 1954), p. 94.

Whose Church?

He saith unto them, But whom say ye that I am? And Simon Peter answered and said, Thou art the Christ, the Son of the living God. And Jesus answered and said unto him, Blessed art thou, Simon Bar-jona: for flesh and blood hath not revealed it unto thee, but my Father which is in heaven. And I say also unto thee, That thou art Peter, and upon this rock I will build my church; and the gates of hell shall not prevail against it. (Matthew 16:15-18)

As I recall, I had not been at the church long when he and I engaged in conversation about churches in general and the church of which we were members in particular. He was a prominent member of the church and had been for some years. He was a leader in the community, respected in the larger area, and a man with money.

In the course of our conversation, we talked about how some folks leave their churches over sharp differences of opinion. "Nobody will ever make me leave *my* church," I remember him saying. I guess I should have picked up on the ominous undertone of the words, but I had no way of knowing how prophetic the statement would turn out to be.

Several years later, I learned that indeed, the church was "his church," for all intents and purposes. He wielded tremendous power, and other "leaders" in the church took their cues from him. I have an idea that as long as he remains there, it will be his church.

The man who made the emphatic statement is not the only one to use it and to accent the word "my." I have known other people in other churches who in various ways carved out their niches of power and who still guard those niches jealously. Some of these people make no attempt to be subtle in calling the shots, influencing decisions, and manipulating people. Others work behind the scenes—and under the table—so that they take minimal chances and never set themselves up for criticism; someone else speaks for them, but the messages are dictated carefully.

In his dramatic statement in Matthew 16, Jesus emphasized that he would build *his* church, the new people of God. He gave himself to redeem all people who will respond to him. He calls people to salvation, to become members of his community. And he lives in his people, whom Paul called the body of Christ. The church is *his* church. Every local expression of Christ's body is his. Only as people follow his leadership do they comprise a church doing his work, continuing his ministry in his world.

Our phrase "belonging to the church" has an important element of truth in it. We belong to a group of people who have a claim on us by virtue of our sharing a common life and a common task. We are partners in a magnificent enterprise. We belong to Christ first of all. Then we belong to his people.

When people adopt the attitude that a church belongs to them because of what they do in it, because of the length of time that they have been a part of it, because of what they give to it in terms of leadership or money, they and "their church" are in trouble. They have lost the proper concept of what being part of Christ's body means. The church has become an arena where power moves are made at the expense of unsuspecting people who have been made pawns in a grim and pathetic game.

The power broker reminded me—and goes on reminding me—that a true church belongs to Christ and follows him. I also belong to Christ and to those who claim him as Lord. I can't afford to forget that.

> *Lord, go on reminding me that the church of which I am part is in no sense mine and that it does not belong to any other person or group, no matter how powerful and influential the individual or the power structure may be. Help me to answer to the Lord of the church. Enable me to see clearly that a majority vote does not always indicate your will, that the church is not a democracy but a theocracy where you rule.*
>
> *When I say "my church," may I have behind the phrase the clear concept, not of ownership, but of fellowship in worship and ministry. Remind me that my participation comes from your gracious invitation to life and to life together with others numbered among your people.*
>
> *In the name of him who loved his church and gave himself for it, Amen.*

The Piano Problem

Only let your conversation be as it becometh the gospel of Christ: that whether I come and see you, or else be absent, I may hear of your affairs, that ye stand fast in one spirit, with one mind striving together for the faith of the gospel. (Philippians 1:27)

I had read and heard hilarious accounts of churches which almost had split over trivial matters, such as what colors were to be used in redecorating, whether or not to buy a new organ to replace a memorial instrument down to its last gasp, whose names were to be placed on stained glass windows, or what kind of sign was to be put in front of the church. Then, as a pastor, I found myself in the middle of one of those situations, and I didn't find anything to laugh at. Now, as I look back, I can smile. At the time, I failed to see any humor at all in a potentially divisive situation.

The church had voted to buy a new piano, and a committee was appointed to bring a recommendation of the kind of instrument that would be best for the church at the best possible price. The committee did its homework and suggested that we buy a Steinway at a reasonable price. The church agreed. So the piano was purchased.

When the beautiful instrument was delivered, it was placed where the old piano had been stationed. We discovered, however, that positioned near one of two rear entrances from a back hallway into the church auditorium, the piano would open into a wall. The instrument's fine, quality sound would be absorbed by the wall rather than being directed out toward the worshiping congregation. We repositioned the piano; in so doing, we blocked the entrance/exit. No matter. Another entrance/exit was on the other side of the auditorium a short distance away. We could use the one passageway instead of the two to which we were accustomed.

Almost immediately, the rumblings started. Some of our church people had used that passageway for years; they wanted the piano repositioned forthwith to clear the way. The piano remained where it was. The rumblings grew. Finally, summoning all the courage I had, I explained to an assembly of adults who were most directly involved in the problem of the blocked passageway that nobody was taking away deliberately a convenient exit. The piano was positioned so that we could take full advantage of its beautiful sound. I think the ice was broken when, as I finished, I turned to leave—toward the exit blocked by the piano. I smiled through my embarrassment, shrugged, and left by the other exit. We all would have to adjust to the change and grow accustomed to a new arrangement.

For weeks, and then months, the most pressing topic of conversation by a good number of church folks had been the piano problem: the positioning of an instrument to everybody's satisfaction. The experience has remained for me a classic example of how easily many of us can become caught up in the trivial at the expense of the really crucial. If that kind of concern had been given to visitation of prospective church members, encouragement of lagging members of the congregation, and ministry to genuine needs, then lives would have been changed and a community would have felt the impact of a caring church.

We easily can become involved in wasting time and energy within the church on matters of little or no real consequence. In fact, we can escape the demanding work of difficult service by staging pitched battles over small things. With all the Goliaths of our time hurling their challenges to the small minority of the truly committed Christians, we don't need to be jousting with each other in our carpeted arenas.

Lord, I don't always distinguish well those things that are crucial from those things that are trivial. Often, I allow my priorities to become confused—or reversed. Help me to see clearly what—and who—is most important in my day-to-day experience. May I not waste precious time and energy on the unimportant, unproductive, trifling matters in my life.

I really want to keep you at the forefront of my priorities, followed by your purpose, my family, other persons, and my country. I will need your assistance in beating back the encroachment of the trivial.

In the name of the One who never allowed the trivial to push aside the crucial, Amen.

4

"Bring . . . the Books"
(2 Timothy 4:13)

Every now and then, during the course of my childhood, teen years, college and seminary experiences, and professional career, I have been introduced to books that have had significant impact on my life. The Bible continues to surprise and amaze me with its light for my path when I really "dig in" and seek its inspired insights. It is foundational, a book set apart from all other books. In addition to Scripture, books written by sensitive, competent people have opened up new horizons for me.

One of the genuine joys of my journey to this point has been to discover books that so captured my response that they demanded my reading them. Some books have been so interesting and have addressed me so directly where I was at a particular time in life that I could not wait for some moments in my day when I could resume reading them. The writers of these books, some of them long dead, have spoken to me in such a way that I have gained new insights into myself, other people, my world, and my role. I have been able to assimilate some of what they have shared so that I have become a better person, a more effective minister.

Consistently, I have attempted to give credit for ideas that were not original with me. In this section, I have tried to share some of the statements and ideas of writers who positively affected my thinking and who helped me to find my way. These are not all of the writers who helped me to get my bearings or who affirmed my direction. I could not include them all, for their names are legion.

Facing Second — or Third — Choices

In Gibeon the Lord appeared to Solomon in a dream by night: and God said, Ask what I shall give thee.

. . . .

*Give therefore thy servant an understanding heart to
judge thy people, that I may discern between good and
bad: for who is able to judge this thy so great a people?
And the speech pleased the Lord, that Solomon had
asked this thing. And God said unto him, Because thou
hast asked this thing, and hast not asked for thyself long
life; neither hast asked riches for thyself, nor hast asked
the life of thine enemies; but hast asked for thyself understanding to discern judgment; behold, I have done according to thy words: lo, I have given thee a wise and an
understanding heart; so that there was none like thee
before thee, neither after thee shall any arise like unto
thee. (1 Kings 3:5,9-12)*

One of the finest sermons I have read is contained in the book
Riverside Sermons, written by Harry Emerson Fosdick. The title of
the sermon is "Handling Life's Second Bests." Seldom—if ever—
have I read or heard anything else that touched me where I live as
those words did when I read them for the first time. Their impact
continues in my journey as a person. I have tried to figure out a way
to preach the major thrust of that marvelous sermon without being
guilty of plagiarizing, but to this point I have been unable to do so.
The words were written years ago, but they speak to me in my present struggle to deal with my experiences and situations in a healthy
manner. They have made possible for me a needed perspective
on—and approach to—decisions with which I am faced.

Only a few of us go through life getting our first choices consistently. Most of us find ourselves with our second choices, or our
third, or with choices even farther down the ladder. We start out
with lofty goals, burning ambitions. We run into a few blank walls,
take a few false trails, encounter some manipulative people who
wield power ruthlessly. For any number of reasons, we are forced
to adjust our goals, alter our dreams. And when we realize that our
first choice is unobtainable, out of the question, we stand at a crucial juncture in our living.

In high school, I dreamed of becoming a coach someday. I was,
and am, anything but an athlete, but I had a passionate love affair
with sports. That dream didn't work out. Down the road, looking
back, I understand why. My first preference was to attend the Uni-

versity of Mississippi. From the time that I first discovered football, I became a Rebel at heart. That dream didn't materialize. During my long stint in seminary, I longed to serve as pastor of a small church. The opportunity never came. A great deal of my life has been spent in dealing with second choices, second bests. (As she reminds me firmly, my wife is one of my happy exceptions.) For too long, I failed to realize that what I do with my second, third, fourth choices is a real test of the stuff of which I am made.

Solomon, king of Israel, chose wisely. He could have chosen anything. He chose wisdom first. Not only did he get that first choice, he received lesser choices: riches and honor. If he lived according to God's demands, he could have a fourth choice: long life. Not many of us can identify with his experience.

When we don't get our first choices, what is our response? Do we pout and indulge in self-pity, with a nothing-ever-works-out-for-me whine? Do we wallow in defeat, failure, or self-loathing? Do we give up on ourselves, on other people, on God? Or do we work to the best of our abilities with whatever choice is available to us? The answer is of critical importance. It tells us a lot we need to know about ourselves.

> *Lord, when I don't get my first choice, something I have my heart set on, let me be able to adjust and to make the most of the choices I have. And let me do so without bitterness or anger. With a dogged determination to make my lesser choice as fulfilling as possible with the help of your grace, help me to forge ahead.*
>
> *In the name of him who didn't always get his first choice, Amen.*

On Being Imperfect

And why beholdest thou the mote that is in thy brother's eye, but considerest not the beam that is in thine own eye? (Matthew 7:3)

Not as though I had already attained, either were already perfect: but I follow after, if that I may apprehend that for which also I am apprehended of Christ Jesus. (Philippians 3:12)

For that which I do I allow not: for what I would, that do I not; but what I hate, that do I. (Romans 7:15)

Be ye therefore perfect, even as your Father which is in heaven is perfect. (Matthew 5:48)

We human beings are a curious lot, to say the least. We do some strange thinking. We do some odd things. For instance, when we finally come to the point where our confessions that we are imperfect are more than words, we find ways to excuse and rationalize our imperfections—while continuing to demand that others be perfect.

Frequently, churches demand this perfection of pastors. Pastors must be proficient in every area of a church's program. They must anticipate and meet the varying needs of the congregation. They must never reveal feet of clay.

On the other hand, pastors often expect a kind of perfection from congregations. People ought to anticipate their pastors' needs and move to meet them. Congregations ought to be enthusiastically responsive to pastoral suggestions. Churches should meet or surpass goals set by their pastors (which subsequently can be used as evidence of pastoral proficiency).

This kind of thinking frequently prevails in marriages, wider family circles, and friendships. Imperfect people expect perfection, and they do not find it. Often, we demand that other people meet our lofty standards while we expect to be excused for coming up short. We expect grace and refuse—or are reluctant—to give it.

I have been helped to see that everything boils down to whether we can live, work, worship, and play together as imperfect people. In our communities, churches, families, and friendships, can we see flaws, deficiencies, and failures, and still live together in openness and acceptance? Can we make our mistakes, allow other people to make theirs, and go on making our way together? Can we really give a margin for imperfection while extending a love that seeks the best for others—with risk and sometimes at cost? The answers are crucial, for they will determine the quality of our relationships.

Tom Mullen hit at something vital in his book *Parables for Parents and Other Original Sinners.* Children and parents will be happier together if they don't expect perfection but accept life together like a picnic—insects along with the treats.

Picnics have ants. People have flaws, and they make honest mistakes. My deep feeling is that we all would enjoy life—and each other—more if we could accept one another for what we are, imperfections and all. We are persons moving toward the goal we see in what we understand of God. We struggle toward his perfection together. None of us has arrived yet.

Lord, I need a healthy tolerance for other people. Sometimes, I expect too much from those around me. And I sometimes mete out justice to others and expect grace for myself. Help me to allow others to be less than perfect, to fail, and to disappoint me without my writing them off. And help me to work on my imperfections before I try to deal with what I perceive as imperfections in others.

In the name of the One who alone was perfect but who accepted imperfect people, Amen.

Lonely Fortresses

I watch, and am as a sparrow alone upon the house top. Mine enemies reproach me all the day; and they that are mad against me are sworn against me. (Psalm 102:7-8)

The prayer is a beautiful expression of one woman's struggle to meet Jesus' difficult demand to love her neighbor. It is a prayer of awesome honesty and insight in *Mockingbirds and Angel Songs & Other Prayers,* written by Jo Carr and Imogene Sorley. The person praying has tried repeatedly to love another who is neighbor because she is encountered in life's traffic. The neighbor keeps resisting all overtures, refusing every offer of friendship with rudeness and even hostility. Then comes the line that stands out to me and demands my reflection: "But I know it's a lonely fortress from which she looks out . . . on an alien world." Life made into a fort to be defended against an environment seen as wholly hostile and people who are enemies or potential enemies—can it actually happen?

I really never had thought about it much, but since reading the prayer I can't get away from the thought. The truth of the penetrating statement has become undeniable to me. It has helped me to understand to a greater degree some of the people I find difficult— or impossible—to love. I know some people who have made their lives lonely fortresses. I remember vividly one pereon in particular who moves defiantly behind walls of bitterness, whose whole stance toward life is negative, hard, and harsh.

Life is what we make it, the cliché goes, and some of us are in the process of making our lives solitary forts which keep people out—and at the same time lock us in. Fortresses have a way of becoming prisons. For some, the eyes well may be mirrors of the soul; but for others, the eyes are peepholes for scanning the terrain, rifle slits through which the enemy may be observed and measured.

I am helped somewhat to realize that many who lash out, who hate, who are hostile, bitter, and hard are fighting defensive battles from solitary positions behind high, thick walls. And I am sobered somewhat by the awareness that it can happen to me. I can't drop all my defenses. I will retain and continue to employ them. They will go up quickly when I sense threat. But I don't want my life to be a lonely fortress from which I look out—fearfully, longingly, and angrily. I want my life to be my house in which I am so increasingly at home that I can invite others in, delighting in their acceptance and living with their refusal. The great thing is that I have a choice.

The alternative is to meet people—as I read somewhere—as potential friends. We can give people the benefit of the doubt, see them as possible allies and sharers in our journey. Some will hurt us and disappoint us. Many more will add touches of richness to our lives.

The possibility exists that with God's help, our lives can become welcome oases in other people's lonely desert stretches. Fortresses or oases—we have a choice.

Lord, I really do want to live in a realistic openness. I
want to meet people with a readiness to relate. And I

don't want to allow those who disappoint me and misuse
me to cause me to retreat into mistrust. I don't want to
live defensively. Help me not to enclose myself behind
walls of anger or hate. And may I not cause anyone else
to make life into an armed camp.

In the name of the One who called—and calls—people
out of lonely fortresses to meaningful community,
Amen.

The Ministry of Approving

*And when Saul was come to Jerusalem, he assayed to
join himself to the disciples: but they were all afraid of
him, and believed not that he was a disciple. But Barnabas took him, and brought him to the apostles, and
declared unto them how he had seen the Lord in the
way, and that he had spoken to him, and how he had
preached boldly at Damascus in the name of Jesus. (Acts
9:26-27)*

One imperative for Christians in our day, our society, it seems to
me, is that we broaden our concept of ministry. In addition to thinking in terms of service to the company of believers, evangelism,
missions, and social action, we need to turn our attention to some
intangibles whose effects sometimes are difficult to measure. Ministry includes such efforts as listening, being present to people,
accepting, and affirming. The more I turn my imagination loose,
the more areas of ministry I discover—and the less I can use the
excuse that I am talentless. Numerous significant, meaningful ministries are open to us in which the most limited persons in the Christian community can be involved.

Wayne Oates, in his book *Confessions of a Workaholic,* has
pointed to a ministry that sensitive Christians can—and must—
perform. "A person can approve himself," Oates has written, "but
he needs another who validates that approval." Many who out-
wardly appear smooth, confident, and secure are struggling in-
wardly for self-approval. We can tell them repeatedly that God
approves of them as persons. But until approval is incarnated in our

relating to them, many people will not be convinced of their worth.

We cannot approve everybody. Not all characters, acts, and attitudes merit our approval. But around us are some people who are involved seriously in a struggle to make progress toward maturity, to live out their redemption in the arenas of their world, to make something of themselves. We can approve these people. We can validate their positive feelings of self-worth. We can give to them a needed intangible.

Paul was having a rough time trying to gain credibility with the disciples in Jerusalem. He had been converted; he had begun to preach. He was trying to live down his past and to live up to his high calling. Barnabas went out on a limb for Paul. He brought Paul into the disciples' circle. Paul forever owed Barnabas a great debt. By his gesture of acceptance and approval, one man helped another in his journey.

The ministry of approving will not win us a plaque, citation, or headline. Such acts won't even gain us honorable mention. No place is given for reporting such ministry in a table of statistics. The effects will be recorded in the lives of people who receive encouragement in their pilgrimages and who perhaps go on to approve others. We receive the developing ability to make personal, concrete, and believable God's approval of persons. And, after all, that is enough.

> *Lord, you once told your disciples that as they had received freely, they were to give freely. Only fairly recently have I been made aware that I have received a great deal of approval and have given too little approval to people around me who deserve it. Help me to affirm the serious efforts of courageous people whose lives I view. Enable me to approve their faithfulness, their graciousness, their gifts, and their care. I can do this only when I sense your approval of me and my efforts, and you can approve me only when I am open to you. Continue to shape me after your likeness as I struggle to give life to you anew each day.*
>
> *In the name of him whose approval means everything, Amen.*

The Importance of Intercession

Praying always with all prayer and supplication in the Spirit, and watching thereunto with all perseverance and supplication for all saints; and for me, that utterance may be given unto me, that I may open my mouth boldly, to make known the mystery of the gospel. (Ephesians 6:18-19)

I thank my God upon every remembrance of you, always in every prayer of mine for you all making request with joy. (Philippians 1:3-4)

One of our cardinal Baptist doctrines is the priesthood of the believer. My impression is that much more is involved in this teaching than we normally explore and implement. Most of us like to emphasize that the concept of the priesthood of the believer means that each Christian can approach God directly and intimately for himself or herself. The other side of that coin is that we go from God's presence to represent him to the people around us. And part of our privilege of addressing God as children talking with a loving, caring, attentive Father is that we can intercede for our fellows: we can place other persons before God.

In his book *Life Together,* Dietrich Bonhoeffer wrote words worth our pondering: "A Christian fellowship lives and exists by the intercession of its members for one another, or it collapses."[1] He defined intercession as our bringing a brother into God's presence, viewing our neighbor as a person in need of grace.

Now, I wish I knew all of the implications of intercessory prayer. I don't. Questions exist to which I have no ready answers. I do not understand all that is involved in, or all that results from, placing another person in God's presence. In times of crisis for those nearest to me and others in my awareness, I simply have placed people before God and have asked him to do what he could do and knew to be best for all persons concerned.

Two things I do know for certain about intercessory prayer. The first is that I cannot pray sincerely for another person—I cannot bring him or her into God's presence—and remain unchanged. I cannot lift another person up before God and casually tear that person apart verbally outside times of prayer. I cannot pray for another individual without being willing for God to use me to answer my own prayer. And I cannot pray genuinely for another person without growing a little in the true humanness that feels for other human beings. When I intercede seriously for my brother or sister, something happens to *me*.

The second thing that I know for sure about intercessory prayer is that I am helped by knowing that someone else cares enough about me to pray for me. When someone says, "I am praying for you," that individual is offering himself or herself as one who is willing to support me and to share my experience.

A scene, still vivid in my memory, will stay with me through life. The lady has been dead for a number of years now, but for several years I was her pastor. She once had been active in her church, serving as a teacher for a number of years. Then, a heart ailment severely limited her activity; for the most part, she was confined to her home. One day, after a brief visit in her home, I was preparing to leave. As she was seeing me out of her house, she told me that she looked forward to getting the church mailout each week. She said that the first thing she did when the church paper came was to look for the sermon topics for the approaching Sunday. Then, she said, she prayed for me. I was touched deeply. I never will forget what it meant to me to know that at least one person brought me into God's presence before I attempted the awesome job of sharing the good news.

We *can* go to God for ourselves. And we have the marvelous opportunity of placing other people in God's presence through our prayers for them.

> *Lord, forgive me for centering my prayers too often and too much on myself. I have legitimate needs that I express to you, as you want me to do. But my selfish requests sometimes dominate when I talk with you. So much so that I don't place enough of my brothers and sisters before you. Often, I don't widen the circle of my concern enough. Move me to a new awareness of the awesome privilege that I have to intercede for others. And*

*may I rise from intercessory prayer to do what I can to be
part of the answer to my prayer.
In the name of the One who even interceded for those
who took his life, Amen.*

Note

1. Dietrich Bonhoeffer, *Life Together* (New York: Harper & Row, Publishers, Inc., 1954), p. 86.

Channeling Aggressiveness

*For ye have heard of my conversation in time past in the
Jews' religion, how that beyond measure I persecuted
the church of God, and wasted it: and profited in the
Jews' religion above many my equals in mine own
nation, being more exceedingly zealous of the traditions
of my fathers. (Galatians 1:13-14)*

*Though I might also have confidence in the flesh. If any
other man thinketh that he hath whereof he might trust in
the flesh, I more: . . . concerning zeal, persecuting the
church. (Philippians 3:4,6a)*

Harry Emerson Fosdick, that prolific preacher-writer whose ministry spanned so many periods of change in our country and who spoke so well and so directly to the concerns of several generations, used a delightfully suggestive term. He spoke and wrote of the right use of "pugnacity." By that word, he meant aggressiveness, the ability of people to assert themselves, to go after something or somebody. I like that word. To me, it immediately conjures up a mental picture of a bulldog ready to attack or to defend with fierce tenacity. Everyone has tenacity, the drive and determination to stay with something until we work it out. Each of us is aggressive to some degree, in some way. The vital question concerns the harnessing of what Fosdick called the "fighting spirit."

Aggressiveness can be—and often is—expressed in wrong ways. It comes out in a cantankerous, quarreling spirit—a readiness to take offense, to rip into people, to display temper. It takes the form of nurtured anger, hatred nursed along. It surfaces in a self-centered grasping. Undisciplined aggressiveness issues in violence. This capacity, placed in us for positive purposes, can become distorted, disruptive, and destructive—in families, churches, work groups, and communities.

Paul was an extremely aggressive, pugnacious man. He certainly possessed a "fighting spirit." Before his conversion, his aggressiveness was directed toward Christians in the form of a searing hatred. After his marvelous experience on the Damascus road, Paul's pugnacity, his fighting spirit, was expressed in his sharing the good news over a wide area of his world despite incredible hardships.

The thought takes shape periodically, especially when I notice negative aggressiveness in me or in other persons: What if the aggressiveness we display too often in destructive, demeaning ways could be applied positively? What difference would be noticeable in us, our families, our churches, our working relationships, our communities? What if we deliberately set out to become aggressive in kindness, in mercy, in unselfishness, in genuine care? What if we really worked at provoking each other to love and good works, as the author of Hebrews put it so well (Heb. 10:24)?

We really have a choice, you and I. And it is a crucial choice. We can use our aggressiveness, our "pugnacity," wholesomely and creatively, or we can use it destructively. We can channel our "fighting spirit" or refuse to discipline it. But we are responsible for our use of a capacity with fine potential.

Lord, I confess what you already know: Sometimes— a great deal of the time—I am aggressive in the wrong way. I am passively aggressive, or I meet aggressiveness with aggressiveness, or I have the wrong goals or purposes behind my aggressiveness. Help me to understand others' mischanneled pugnacity and to deal with it in a healthy way. Enable me to direct my fighting spirit for high purposes. I don't want to lose it; I want to use it well. Help me to do so in your Spirit. In the name of him who had a marvelous fighting spirit and who used it correctly every time, Amen.

Levels of Response

*Therefore all things whatsoever ye would that men
should do to you, do ye even so to them: for this is the
law and the prophets. (Matthew 7:12)*

Years ago, I heard it said in jest—a twist of the "golden rule" not
so humorous to those people who have had it applied to them. "Do
unto others before they have a chance to do unto you," the not-so-
golden rule went. Some individuals actually do spend a great deal
of time getting the jump on other people, using and manipulating
them in anticipation of those people trying the same tactics at first
opportunity. This is one level of response open to us in our living.
For some of us, it is our prevailing response.

Colin Morris, in his book *The Hammer of the Lord,* points to
three other levels of response which we can adopt. We can do to
others as they have done to us: good for good, bad for bad. We can
take the stance of retribution; in so doing, we can let vindictive,
insensitive people control our primary way of responding.

We can do to others as we would like for them to do to us. Morris
calls this the "ethics of optimism," an approach often quickly dis-
couraged as goodwill encounters repeated evil.

Or, we can do to others as Christ has done to us. This law distills
the issue of the gospel; these are the ethics of hope. According to
Morris, this level of response demands a willingness to offer our fellows what Christ has offered to us: sacrifice, acceptance, and re-
newal through suffering.

We can choose our level of response—no matter what our back-
grounds are, no matter what our present contexts may be, no matter what may be the level of response of people with whom we
interact. To allow others to determine our response is tragic; to go
through life reacting instead of responding in a well thought out
manner is sad. To choose with the help of Christ is liberating
beyond description.

We can see people as competitors, potential enemies, and "wire
work" them first. We can demand an eye for an eye or mete out
favors in exact measure of good done to us. We can use our own
preferences as a standard by which we treat others. Or, we can

work to adopt the stance of Christ—a stance of firmness and fairness. Which level of response will contribute most to our struggle to become persons marked by maturity? Which level most clearly views others as persons of worth? I think I know.

Lord, I have an idea that I spend too much of my time reacting rather than acting or responding in a mature, intelligent manner. And I am afraid that most of my reacting—and my more infrequent responses—are done in kind. I know that I should respond to people as you respond to me, and in my best moments I want to do that. But, as Paul wrote, I am not able to do the good that I would do. Not nearly often enough. Help me to be secure and unselfish enough to respond as you do, meeting evil with an overplus of good, loving and praying for enemies, refusing to retaliate, not limiting good acts to those who have done me good. That kind of responding is not easy. But, then, you never said that it was.

In the name of the One who always responded in a manner that was best for others, Amen.

A Liberating Lesson

My days are past, my purposes are broken off, even the thoughts of my heart. (Job 17:11)

Take therefore no thought for the morrow: for the morrow shall take thought for the things of itself. Sufficient unto the day is the evil thereof. (Matthew 6:34)

Better late than never. Better to learn the lesson at age forty than never to have learned it. The teacher was Sam Keen in his book, *To a Dancing God.* He wrote about his being an exile for too many years, trying to live in the past or in the future and thereby being an exile from the present—by choice. I was with him as I read line after line. In his experience, I could see something of myself.

Two sentences really struck home: "After squandering much of my substance wandering in the future and the past I was returning to my native time—the present. I had not yet learned how to cultivate the now, to live gracefully in the present, to love the actual, but I was no longer in exile."[1] I began to reflect on the question of where I was spending most of my time, and I learned a little about myself.

Every now and then, I have to remind myself to maintain a healthy attitude toward what is past. My past is mine—good and bad, positive and negative, right and wrong, pleasure and pain, success and failure. It remains a part of me in the sense that I can continue to use it, to glean from it lessons and materials that help me now. But I can't spend a great deal of my time rummaging around in a past that I cannot change.

My future is open. I can plan, project, hope, and dream where I cannot see clearly or know for sure. But I must guard against twin threats about my future. I must avoid the overanxiety concerning tomorrow about which Jesus warned. Neither can I play pretend with myself, always thinking that the next place, the next job will be the greenest pasture I could want.

What I have of greatest value is now, a present loaded with possibilities and pressures, amusements and agonies, opportunities and dead-end streets. And I am responsible for myself—for how I use my past, for the way I go to meet my future. Most of all, I am responsible for what I make of today, right now.

Somehow, I have the feeling that I have been set free—free from blaming other people for past difficulties and from wallowing in carried-over guilt; free from the tendency to look at some future accomplishment, acquisition, or "break" to bring me an elusive fulfillment. I sense a new freedom to enjoy today, to take whatever it brings and to make the most of it, to celebrate life with those who share mine most intimately. I don't feel any "tomorrow may never come" fatalism. Hopefully, I won't throw away the past or ignore the future. I would like to invest most of my energy in my present. To me, that is good stewardship, and as Christian as anything I can do.

Lord, I have been guilty of incredible waste. I have spent far too much time and mental and emotional en-

ergy in the past and in a fancied future. Often, I have not been present to the now, and I have let golden opportunities slip by me. I haven't seen people, or heard them, or helped them. I haven't shared meaningful time with my wife and children. I haven't given a particular today to you. I have cheated myself, you, and other people.

I will need your help in learning to live each day to the full, making maximum use of it. Help me to live in the present without being pulled apart by the tension of a past and a future tugging in opposite directions.

In the name of him who never was an exile from his present, Amen.

Note

1. Sam Keen, *To a Dancing God* (New York: Harper & Row, Publishers, Inc.), p. 21.

Dominant Desire

That I may know him, and the power of his resurrection, and the fellowship of his sufferings, being made conformable unto his death. (Philippians 3:10)

Pray without ceasing. (1 Thessalonians 5:17)

Several years ago, I ran across an idea that I hoped to develop into a sermon on prayer one day. I never worked up the sermon, but the concept continues to intrigue me. In his book, *The Meaning of Prayer*, Harry Emerson Fosdick wrote that in an inclusive sense, the settled craving of an individual's life, his or her inward love and determining desire, is that person's real prayer. Whatever prevailing claim we place on life, that is our prayer. And a person has a way of marshaling the forces of life, consciously and unconsciously, in the direction of satisfying that dominant desire.

Immediately, this concept—new to me—forced me to begin probing for the dominant desire in my life. I began the effort to get in touch with what I really wanted for myself and others *no matter what my carefully worded prayers had been conveying.* I still have to ask myself some tough questions. Do I want to be successful in living a quality life of developing character, or do I want to be seen and known as a success in the particular role that I have chosen? Do I actually want to share with other people on a level of depth, or do I want to win their admiration and affirmation by a shallow, pretended interest in them? Do I desire to give, or to accumulate; to care for, or to be taken care of; to relate in honesty, or to manipulate and use other people? Beyond my words and my carefully framed religious thoughts, what is the constant prayer my life expresses to God?

To realize that life ultimately is measured by its dominant desire is sobering. We become what we think in our hearts, what we will consistently and determinedly. Therefore, that we identify clearly our dominant desires is imperative. We must bring out into the light of day what we want most of all and call it by its right name. Then, we must place dominant desire in the light of God's revelation of himself in Jesus of Nazareth and allow those desires to be affirmed or redeemed. We will need all the courage God can give us to identify the dominant demand that we are placing on life—and that many of us are keeping well hidden behind our words.

Lord, give me the courage to probe the depths of my life and to identify the dominant desire that I find there. As far as I can know myself, I want to be a person becoming more of what I know you to be. I want to be moving toward filling up the pattern that I see in Christ. And I want to be one who can feel deeply for and with others.

But I also am aware that many of my dominant desires have to do with myself in a selfish way. To get, to achieve, to be recognized—these desires sometimes are strong. I don't want them to crowd out the better drives, the nobler desires. Create within me a clean heart, a new spirit—and the strong desire to have you shape my life.

In the name of the One whose dominant desire was to do the will of his Father, Amen.

"Meanwhile Ministry"

And they came to Jericho: and as he went out of Jericho with his disciples and a great number of people, blind Bartimaeus, the son of Timaeus, sat by the highway side begging. And when he heard that it was Jesus of Nazareth, he began to cry out, and say, Jesus, thou Son of David, have mercy on me. And many charged him that he should hold his peace: but he cried the more a great deal, Thou Son of David, have mercy on me. And Jesus stood still, and commanded him to be called. And they call the blind man, saying unto him, Be of good comfort, rise; he calleth thee. (Mark 10:46-49)

But a certain Samaritan, as he journeyed, came where he was: and when he saw him, he had compassion on him, and went to him, and bound up his wounds, pouring in oil and wine, and set him on his own beast, and brought him to an inn, and took care of him. (Luke 10:33-34)

Halford Luccock has written something highly suggestive to me. In his exposition on the Gospel of Mark in *The Interpreter's Bible*, he has shared some remarkable insights in applying Scripture to life. In commenting on Jesus' healing of the blind beggar Bartimaeus, recorded in Mark 10, Luccock observed: "It is the 'meanwhile' mercy, the roadside ministries, that we are so apt to omit. We are absorbed in a task, and the deeds of helpfulness which have no relation to it, which contribute nothing to forward it, seem trivial. . . . There is sometimes a disdain for 'meanwhile' ministries."[1]

As I ponder Luccock's words, I recall some words of Jesus. He told a story about a man who was robbed, beaten, and left for dead—or to die—by the road. Two religious types approached, looked, and passed by on the other side of the road. A Samaritan, a "nobody" as far as Jews were concerned, happened along. This unlikely hero stopped and helped. Now, what bothers me is that as much as I would like to identify with the Samaritan, I see a strong resemblance to two religious figures who served in their religious

functions but who evidently had no sensitivity, no time, and no inclination for "meanwhile ministry." I am a religious type, but I travel
various roads in my daily and weekly doings. And I am not nearly
as good as I would like to be—as I need to be—at roadside mercy. I
need for the words of Jesus to remind me periodically that it is outside my temples—where I work and live and worship—that I encounter people by the side of their roads. Each time I encounter
one of life's victims, my life is tested.

We were shopping in a large department store. I heard the child
crying before I saw her. A lady was stooping to comfort the little girl
who had become separated from her mother. The lady began dry-
ing the child's tears. She took a small hand in hers and assured the
child that together they would find the mother. I am sure that the
woman was as much in a hurry as the rest of the shoppers in the
store. But a little girl was worth stopping for, worth the time and
effort it would take to reunite her with her mother. That act has
remained an acted parable for me. Persons, no matter who they
are, are worth turning aside for, stopping for. And I have the nagging feeling that these "meanwhile ministries" are more of a test of
what we are than any planned, organized acts of service.

And that thought shakes me some. I am forced to ask again:
How much do I care for people I encounter on my roads to multiple
goals, especially those who call to me on my way by or who are victims? "Meanwhile ministry" may offer me the best opportunity to
express the love of Christ in concrete, meaningful, and effective
ways. I have found the concept something to think about.

> *Lord, how many people have I passed who were lying
> by the sides of the various roads that I have traveled?
> Too busy, too preoccupied, too much in a hurry, too in-
> sensitive to care enough, I have gone on my way. And I
> have failed the real tests of what being truly religious and
> truly human means. Forgive me. For the rest of my jour-
> ney, help me to be aware of those who are victims or
> who have been victimized. Help me to stop and offer
> what I can to help them up and on their way again. Re-
> mind me repeatedly that each opportunity to assist a per-
> son, whether to a large or small degree, tests the quality*

*of my life and the depth of my understanding of what
you require.*

*In the name of the One who was a master at "mean-
while ministry," Amen.*

Note

1. Halford Luccock, *Mark, The Interpreter's Bible*, VII (Nashville: Abingdon
Press, 1951), 822.

Life's Interruptions

*While he spake these things unto them, behold, there
came a certain ruler, and worshipped him, saying, My
daughter is even now dead: but come and lay thy hand
upon her, and she shall live. And Jesus arose, and followed him, and so did his disciples. And, behold, a
woman, which was diseased with an issue of blood
twelve years, came behind him, and touched the hem of
his garment: for she said within herself, If I may but touch
his garment, I shall be whole. (Matthew 9:18-21)*

Basically, I don't care much for interruptions—at the office working; at home reading the newspaper; watching a ball game on television; writing; in conversation with one to whom I am attempting
to minister or with a friend in casual exchange. Interruptions can
foul up a schedule or an orderly flow of life's activities and can
cause a great deal of frustration, irritation, and anxiety.

A few years ago, Dietrich Bonhoeffer reached across the years to
give me a new slant on interruptions. In his book, *Life Together,* he
wrote: "We must be ready to allow ourselves to be interrupted by
God. God will be constantly crossing our paths and canceling our
plans by sending us people with claims and petitions. We may pass
them by, preoccupied with our more important tasks, as the priest
passed by the man who had fallen among thieves, perhaps—
reading the Bible."[1] When I first read those words, I was forced to

ask myself: Could it be that in my pursuits as a pastor, I was brushing off interruptions which offered opportunities to meet another person at the point of legitimate need? All along, to this point in my pilgrimage, have I been failing to make the genuinely human response—while busily and piously reading my Bible?

When my wife and children interrupt me and break my concentration, they may be anything but thoughtless. Their interruptions may be pleas for some of my time, for attention and a needed expression of my care for them. In such unstructured, spontaneous moments, I may be given chances to share in love—chances which never will come again.

Sometimes, when people at work, in the church, or in other places interrupt me, it may not be a lack of respect for my time and agenda. It well may be that some of those individuals are asking to be seen as persons, to be heard as people whose concerns are important. They may be asking for approval and affirmation. Some may be sharing secrets tentatively to determine if I can accept them as they are.

I have spent a great deal of time in unproductive anger and resentment over interruptions. My responses to being distracted from the task at hand are not always what they should be. They are not the creative kind of response that Jesus made to interruptions that he experienced. But I keep working toward the insight necessary to look for the opportunities that sometimes lie just beneath the surface of an interruption.

> *Lord, I confess that most of the time interruptions are unwelcome intrusions on my time and activities. Forgive me for not using them, making them creative experiences. Help me to look for the possibilities of ministry in interruptions. Even when I find none, may I be patient and kind, and in so doing say something about you and your attitude toward people.*
>
> *When I am absorbed in myself or whiling away valuable time, interrupt me with demands and challenges that will stretch my life.*
>
> *In the name of him who used interruptions redemptively, Amen.*

Note

1. Dietrich Bonhoeffer, *Life Together* (New York: Harper & Row, Publishers, Inc., 1954), p. 99.

Open to the New

No man also seweth a piece of new cloth on an old garment: else the new piece that filled it up taketh away from the old, and the rent is made worse. And no man putteth new wine into old bottles: else the new wine doth burst the bottles, and the wine is spilled, and the bottles will be marred: but new wine must be put into new bottles. (Mark 2:21-22)

And he that sat upon the throne said, Behold, I make all things new. (Revelation 21:5)

As I recall, it was the coming of a new year that started me to thinking about it. Something Leslie Weatherhead wrote in his book, *Time for God,* struck a responsive chord: "Jesus Christ said that the greatest commandment was that men should love the Lord their God with all their minds. Surely this means that we are never to close our minds against new truth from whatever source it may come, and never to be more eager to preserve the old and traditional than to welcome the new, once the new has authenticated itself to us in an hour of honest examination."[1] Few of us really want to live in the past, hanging on to yesterday. Yet, I have the feeling that in our religious thinking, many of us attempt to preserve the past intact. Somebody back there said it, or wrote it. Most people give assent to that interpretation. So, that settles it.

Now, some of the things that are "old and traditional" are valuable in our attempts to live well now. We can, and should, glean the good from the past. But the gleaning should be done *as we do our own thinking.*

I am convinced that many people in our time are possessors of "traditional religion." In many cases, this is true, not because we have been forced to agree with certain doctrines, but because we want to please other significant people in our lives. Most often, we possess traditional religion because we do not want to do the difficult work of examining the faith we possess. We hold tightly to unexamined statements and second-hand theology that make little difference in our living because to think for ourselves is demanding work.

Surely God is attempting to give us more light for our way, to lead us into new understanding of his character, purpose, and demands. He spoke his final word of revelation and redemption in his Son. But we haven't arrived at a final interpretation of that Word. We continue to discover new facets of that marvelous personality, facets which speak to us where we are.

The realization that, for the most part, the religious people of Jesus' day were not open to the new he brought frightens me. Most of them clung to a tightly closed, closely guarded system of religion. Everything was worked out carefully; they had God in a box. Jesus came with a refreshing, redemptive revelation of what God is like and what he wants from us. And those protective of their traditions rejected the light and became blind. What this says to me is that now I can refuse to hear the sounds of the new that God is trying to speak. I can close my eyes to the new that God is attempting to show me. I can allow my sensitivity, my intuition, to harden to the point that I cannot feel the new which God would like to impress on me. I can be closed to the new.

I hope and pray that I will be open to the new that I will encounter today and through my tomorrows if I am sensitive to the One who comes to meet me. I would like to be open to new possibilities, new challenges, new opportunities, and new truths. I will try to have the courage to examine that by which I seek to live with a prayer that I will not allow the comfort, safety, and easy way of the unexamined traditional to prevent my being open to the new.

Lord, deep down inside I know that I am capable of being closed to the new. I am comfortable with the familiar. I am lazy and tend to avoid the hard work of clear thinking. I am threatened by change. Sometimes I find that not to see or hear or feel is convenient in maintaining my status quo.

Help me to know — more than intellectually — that you

*have not finished with us yet, that you have more to do.
Help me to pick up on what you are doing and to be willing to be part of it. Enable me to be open to the new that
comes from you.*

*In the name of him who brought something so shock-
ingly new into our world that we never have plumbed its
depths, Amen.*

Note

1. Leslie Weatherhead, *Time for God* (Nashville: Abingdon Press, 1967), p.
71.

On Messing Up

*And Peter answered and said to Jesus, Master, it is good
for us to be here: and let us make three tabernacles; one
for thee, and one for Moses, and one for Elias. For he
wist not what to say; for they were sore afraid. (Mark
9:5-6)*

The words really grabbed my attention. They did for me what I
need quite often: They forced me to do some serious thinking
about myself and my fellow pilgrims. The words formed a brief
prayer in the book, *Mocking Birds and Angel Songs & Other
Prayers,* by Jo Carr and Imogene Sorley. In the prayer, the writer
shared with God a moving experience with her child. The little
seven-year-old girl had written a thank-you letter and had attempted to draw an illustration on the back. The drawing had not turned
out well, so the child had scribbled through it and had written apol-
ogetically: "I misst it up." The writer went on to confess, "Ah,
Father! Me, too!" Then she asked for the ability not to get too down
on herself, since God understands blunders.

Simon Peter "misst it up," on more than one occasion. On the
Mount of Transfiguration, he hastily and unfortunately blurted out a
suggestion before he gave it sufficient thought. Before that, he
attempted to correct Jesus after the Master declared that the Son of
Man would suffer. But we really can't be too rough on Simon. We
all mess up now and then, some of us more frequently than others.

The person I know best seems to have a rare talent for it; I never can say that I have no ability. As a small child, Leigh, in her honest responses I had grown to expect—and sometimes to dread—summed it up well now and then: "You messed up, didn't you, Daddy?" Most of us know what it means to be in error—to speak before we have the facts and before we think a matter through; to act hastily out of surging emotion; to rupture relationships inadvertantly, carelessly; to choose a wrong course in life; to fail to do something well—or adequately. Sometimes, even when we mean well, things go wrong. We find ourselves writing across our experience: "I misst it up."

The realization that God can use our blunders to teach us and that he gives us credit for our motives contains something redemptive and encouraging. If we can learn from our messing up without engaging in extended, morbid self-demeaning, we can move toward maturity. We can grant to ourselves and to those around us the freedom to mess up now and then as part of the human pilgrimage, with a view to helping each other toward recovery. One who is most like a Father helps us to start over again on a new page.

The prodigal in Jesus' story always will remain the classic example of a person who acted rashly out of immaturity, stubbornness, and less-than-clear thinking. Probably, he went against his father's advice. He made a mess of his life. But he learned from the mess he made. His father accepted him without "I told you so's." His father helped him put the shattered pieces of his life together again and to start over. But first, the son had to say to himself—and then to his father—"I misst it up."

The hard truth is that we all mess up to degrees ranging from humorous to serious. The good news is that God understands and is willing to enter our situations and to act creatively on our behalf.

Lord, I never have been to the point that the prodigal—and modern-day prodigals—reached. I never have messed up my life to the degree that I sometimes see and read about. But you and I both know that I "mess up" more than my share. I speak angry words, or fail to be considerate, or decline to do the good that I know to do, or play a role, or think only of myself. Again and again, I am forced to write across a day, an experience, a rela-

tionship, a work task: "I misst it up!"

Thank you that you are a God of new beginnings, fresh starts, second chances. I need clean pages quite frequently.

In the name of the One who never "misst it up" but who has compassion on those of us who do, Amen.

Working My Ground

Then Peter, turning about, seeth the disciple whom Jesus loved following; which also leaned on his breast at supper, and said, Lord, which is he that betrayeth thee? Peter seeing him saith to Jesus, Lord, and what shall this man do? Jesus saith unto him, If I will that he tarry till I come, what is that to thee? follow thou me. (John 21:20-22)

If I had read his incisive words much earlier in life, I could have prevented the rather extensive waste of a great deal of my time and mental and emotional energy. I have encountered a good many people to this point in my pilgrimage, and I have envied some of them. Some of these were, and are, my friends; some of them I didn't like at all. But I looked at them, noted what life had given to them, and envied them. For these who drew my attention were multitalented, gifted, personable, and popular. And I saw myself as almost totally devoid of ability. I often reflected on the poor hand that life had dealt me. Deep inside, I felt the stirrings of anger and frustration. I wish that I had known all along what I have encountered relatively recently.

Somewhere along my way, I picked up, browsed through, and bought a book written by Harry Emerson Fosdick. *On Being a Real Person* marked the start of my debt to this marvelous minister of another generation. He wrote: "Life is a landscaping job. We are handed a site, ample, or small, rugged or flat, picturesque or commonplace, whose general outlines and contours are largely determined for us."[1] We are given one acre, as it were, to see what we can make of it. Some ground is better than other plots, but each person is responsible for using to the fullest extent what he or she has been given. I need to be at work removing the rocks and stumps from my acre so that it is as productive as I can make it; I can't waste time or energy gazing at someone else's more fertile acre. He or she is responsible for what is done with greater potential.

Elizabeth O'Connor phrased the same idea in a different way in her book, *Eighth Day of Creation.* She wrote that when we spend our energy watching others' lives, we have none to expend in fulfilling our own possibilities. Life's wealth can be spent in only one place at a time, never in two. The first place we must apply our currency is on ourselves, finding what we have to offer out of our uniqueness.

The more I have thought about it, the more convinced I have become that a basic Christian demand is that we spend a great deal of time and expend vast energy *on ourselves first.* That has a selfish ring to it, I know. But the self we offer to Christ must be hard at work finding and realizing potential. The self we offer to those around us must be certain of identity, strengths, and worth. We must find and refine our gifts before we can offer them effectively.

All of us are susceptible to the temptation to "life watch." We can gnash our teeth at others' gifts, achievements, positions, and acquisitions. Or, we can do the work of probing ourselves for the good that is there. We can spend our gold at the right place, for the right purpose.

> *Lord, I have squandered too much of the gold you gave me. In envy, self-pity, anger, and frustration, I have despised the plot you gave me while looking at choicer plots around me. Forgive me for taking so long to appreciate what you have given me and to begin the task of making the most of it that you and I can. Work with me each day in making this one little life as productive as possible. Help me to recognize my limitations but also my possibilities, and enable me to major on the potential.*
>
> *In the name of him who made the most of his life and helped others to make the most of theirs, Amen.*

Note

1. Harry Emerson Fosdick, *On Being a Real Person* (New York: Harper & Row Publishers, Inc., 1943), p. 69.

5

"Out of the Mouth of Babes"
(Psalm 8:2)

For years, children have fascinated me. When I began to listen to them, be present to them, encourage them to respond, I increasingly was impressed with their openness, their honest directness, their simple way of looking at things, and expressing themselves. Who they are, what they do, and the things they say can get us in touch with truths we have forgotten or neglected. Their words, I have found, can trigger responses deep within us and can start our thinking along surprising and needed directions.

My children are not exceptionally brilliant. They do not have insights beyond their years. They are normal, active, inquisitive little persons. They can be sources of great delight or of wall-climbing frustration. Some years ago, I realized that if I really listened to them, their unique ways of phrasing their thoughts and questions could channel my thinking along the lines of the ultimates, the lasting values, and the primary qualities in life.

I don't go around giving up-to-the-minute reports on wnat my children have said and done. I don't take over conversations and monopolize people's time to paint Leigh and Jeff bigger than life. On meeting friends, I don't whip out pictures immediately in order to extol my children's beauty and handsomeness. Other people have children who are special to them, and I remain aware of this. My children are normal, healthy little people who are gifts to us for a while—an all-too-brief while. My concern is that I give them as much as I can of the intangibles and the tangibles to help prepare and equip them for their futures. And I hope to continue to learn from them.

In the vignettes which follow, I have recorded some—by no means all—of my children's words that have caused me to do some serious, often hard thinking about myself and about life in general. All children say some things that are profound and probing in their simplicity, directness, and blunt honesty. We don't always hear them, and sometimes we don't let them express themselves freely. I was fortunate enough to be helped to see the value of listening to the two little people with whom I share life. I don't always listen. When I fail to hear them, I am the loser.

Take the following vignettes in the spirit in which they are offered: reflections that were sparked by remarks, studied and offhand, that were not expressions of genius but of developing minds responding to and asking questions about their world. My children's declarations and questions have enriched my life to a surprising degree that I am not able to measure.

Beyond Recall

> *So teach us to number our days, that we may apply our hearts unto wisdom. (Psalm 90:12)*

> *As for man, his days are as grass: as a flower of the field, so he flourisheth. For the wind passeth over it, and it is gone; and the place thereof shall know it no more. (Psalm 103:15-16)*

Leigh and I were returning from a church league softball game in which I had played—after a fashion. She was asking about the game, and I was trying to answer her questions in terms that a not-quite-five-year-old could understand. Quite unexpectedly, she asked why I didn't play football. I coughed, cleared my throat, and finally muttered that football was a game for younger men.

All was quiet for a long moment. Then Leigh asked: "Daddy, when you get young, will you play football then?"

After a brief but awkward pause, I smiled and told her that we don't get young again. Being young is a one-time thing.

Leigh's frank, simple question got me in touch with a truth I already knew. In a fresh, forceful way that sermons, books, and discussions never had been able to do, my daughter made me rethink a fact of life—and death. It was a tough question for a man just turned forty-one and getting in touch with his mortality. It reminded me that the years are getting away for all of us, that life has a limited number of productive years, that powers I take for granted have a way of diminishing. Youth and young adulthood and the middle years rapidly, steadily pass beyond recall. A vital part of living in depth is to make good use of the years given to us, to maintain the attempt to live one day at a time. Time is an elusive, never-before, never-again thing. It is the most valuable gift we are given. It can be squandered on the meaningless, or wasted on the wrong, or invested in the best we know.

I won't play football when I get young again. But the older I get, the more I want to use my years in such a way that I will have more satisfaction than regret when I look back. I would like to live so that the years swiftly moving beyond recall will have been as productive as I could make them. And I want to live well enough that my children have the best guidance and support that I can give them to enable them to enjoy youth and to make it a solid preparation for mature adulthood. I can't call back the years; I never will be able to do so. But I can work to use each one more creatively than the one before.

> *Lord, help me to number my days, to be aware that each one is a treasure that I can spend only once. Help me to know where I am in my life, what time it is with me.*
>
> *Thank you for the days that you have given to me. Some I have spent well. Others I have squandered. Forgive me for the misused days, and help me to use well whatever tomorrows will be mine.*
>
> *In the name of the One who used all his days here to the full, Amen.*

When I Try

I can do all things through Christ which strengtheneth me. (Philippians 4:13)

We were gathered around the table, ready to eat dinner. As our custom is, we held hands around the table and waited for Leigh or Jeff to express thanks to God for the food. On this night, Leigh volunteered quickly. She thanked God for a number of things, including our food. Then, at the close of her prayer, she said something that stunned me: "And thank you, God, for showing me what I can do that I didn't know I could do until I tried." I sat there with my mouth open, looking at her.

To this day, I don't know where Leigh got the idea she expressed so beautifully in her prayer. Perhaps a teacher at school had persisted in her encouragement of Leigh until Leigh did something she had feared she could not do. Maybe Barbara had prodded her until she attempted something new and challenging. Whatever happened, Leigh was introduced to a truth that will serve her well all of her life: Only when we try in the face of possible failure do we stretch our lives.

Possibly, Leigh put into her own words the moral of a story I had read to her innumerable times when she was smaller. She enjoyed hearing about—and seeing the pictures of—the little engine who kept saying, "I think I can," huffing and puffing up a hill. At the top and on the way down the other side, the little engine exclaimed joyfully: "I-thought-I—could." Few things in life compare with the experience of setting out on an adventurous attempt of something new and discovering new abilities, capacities, and gifts.

"Until I tried." Most of us like to play it safe, stay with the familiar, or retreat into the comfortable. Most of the time, to try is exerting, demanding, and even painful. The pitiful fact is that any number of people in various settings in life never will know what they could have done because they did not try.

Years ago, as Boy Scouts, a pal and I were trying to earn our athletic merit badges. The high school coach was to pass us on the baseball throw, the broad jump, and several other requirments. My buddy was a fine little athlete. He would have no trouble. I felt that I could do most of the things I would have to do—except the broad jump. The distance was too great, I felt. I was not a good jumper. The time came for my friend and me to meet our tests. I had decided that I would do the best that I could do and hope (and pray) a lot. If I didn't do something right, I would keep at it until I finally did it. I wouldn't be hurt by trying (except by the laughter of other boys who would watch and would see my futile efforts); and for all I knew, I might get lucky. On my first jump, I soared (if you could call it that) the required distance. My buddy confessed that he never thought I would make it. My guess is that adrenaline played a large part in my feat. You never know until you try—a trite but enduring truth.

I hope that Leigh will face up to the many challenges she will face in life. I hope that she will try her wings, to discover more often than not that she can fly. And I hope that for the rest of my life, I will be given the necessary courage to try, to set off into unknown territory, to attempt the unfamiliar, to take on the demanding. I must be given that courage by One who wants me to stretch my life, to broaden my horizons, to go on discovering new abilities that I didn't know I had—until I tried.

Paul's words to his friends in Philippi offer the encouragement that we need in order to try in the face of possible failure. Literally he wrote: "All things I am strong in the one empowering me" (author's translation). Necessary strength is available for us in our attempting and in our successes and failures. And when we attempt for Christ, he is with us all the way.

Lord, thank you for a child's prayer that made alive for me again a truth by which I need to live. Sometimes, it is easier for me if I don't try the difficult and demanding. I find myself living defensively, trying all I know to avoid failure. Help me to live my life positively, on the offense. Give me grace to try, to give demands and opportunities my best shot and then to move to the next challenge. In the name of the One who never quit trying to express your love and grace, Amen.

What We Want, and What We Get

Then Jesus beholding him loved him, and said unto him, One thing thou lackest: go thy way, sell whatsoever thou hast, and give to the poor, and thou shalt have treasure in heaven: and come, take up the cross, and follow me. And he was sad at that saying, and went away grieved: for he had great possessions. (Mark 10:21-22)

> *And lest I should be exalted above measure through the*
> *abundance of the revelations, there was given to me a*
> *thorn in the flesh, the messenger of Satan to buffet me,*
> *lest I should be exalted above measure. For this thing I*
> *besought the Lord thrice, that it might depart from me.*
> *And he said unto me, My grace is sufficient for thee: for*
> *my strength is made perfect in weakness. (2 Corinthians*
> *12:7-9a)*

Several years ago, Barbara prepared to leave the house to meet a friend downtown for a short shopping foray. Leigh began her campaign to be allowed to go along. Her mother refused her repeated—and at last tearful—pleas and attempted to explain why Leigh couldn't go. After Barbara left, I was faced with the task of dealing with a five-year-old girl's disappointment and a two-year-old boy's boundless energy. Shortly, I overheard Leigh talking to her brother.

"Don't bother me, Jeff," she said sternly. "My allergy problem is giving me trouble, and I can't go where I want to go." I thought of another of her favorite phrases: "I don't *ever* get to do what I want to do."

Leigh was in the process of learning a lesson that comes hard, a lesson that some people never learn: We don't always get the things we want or as much of some things as we would like; we don't always get our way in life's interchanges. My hope is that Barbara and I can help Leigh and Jeff come to a healthy handling of their not getting what they want when they want it.

Most of us have a large range of wants: money, houses, cars, clothes, recognition, affirmation, love, respect. Many of our wants go unmet. As a child growing up, I can remember few things that I really wanted and didn't get: a tribike; a long-barrelled, six-shooter cap gun; a pair of rubber boots for tramping the woods; a pair of baseball shoes. My response to some of these unmet wants was anger and ongoing frustration. Dealing with unmet wants is a key experience constantly repeated for all of us.

What we do when we don't get what we want, or all that we want is a test of maturity, just as is our failure to meet goals and to realize dreams. Children sometimes react by throwing themselves to the floor, crying, and kicking. If the tantrum works, they carry the method on into adolescence and adulthood. And by whatever names we call them, adult responses often are childish tantrums with greater dimensions of rage and greater danger to the objects of that rage. Some people are angry all the time. Life owes them something, an ill-defined something that actually never would be enough. Many people turn their resentment inward and are depressed much of the time. Some adults react to unmet wants by sulking and pouting. They pick up their toys and withdraw.

We can make a healthy response to receiving less than we want, to being unable to go where we would like and to do what we desire. We can work with what is available. We can turn our attention to other areas of worthwhile endeavor. Jesus didn't get everything he wanted. Not everybody responded to him and his message. Paul didn't get everything he wanted. He had to live with his thorn in the flesh. Both went on with their work, making the best of it.

The mature response to unmet wants is to make the best of what we have. In Leigh's case, she worked on a puzzle and then conned me into reading to Jeff and her. A search for ways to compensate sometimes can lead to discovery of gifts, pleasures, and fulfillments that would have remained unclaimed had we received what we wanted in the first place. Not always, but sometimes.

What I want and what I get often will be two different things. I would like to handle both getting and not getting with grace.

> Lord, I have a lot of wants. Some of them are legitimate needs. Many of them are desires for fringes and frills. Help me to want the right things for myself and my family. When I do not get what I want, help me to respond in a mature manner. Help me to avoid pouting, becoming angry, or quitting. Help me to examine the experience in such a way that I learn from it, and enable me to go on without carrying the unnecessary load of frustration.
>
> If I know myself, in my moments of clearest insight I want to have a closer relationship to you, more of your attitude, more of your Spirit. I want to follow your lead-

ing. I want to be more than I am. Somehow, I feel that this is at least part of what you want for me. Help me to cooperate with you so that I get what you want for me. In the name of the One who wants the best for his own, Amen.

No Going Back

So he drove out the man; and he placed at the east of the garden of Eden Cherubims, and a flaming sword which turned every way, to keep the way of the tree of life. (Genesis 3:24)

One night, in Jeff's fifth year of life and my forty-fourth, I was reading him the riot act about the condition of his room. I had bathed him and was helping him put on his pajamas. Around us was what looked like the aftermath of a pitched battle in which two armies had met, struggled, and retreated, leaving the terrain mangled and littered with abandoned equipment and debris. I was leaning on him pretty heavily, and I delivered an ultimatum: He was to clean up his room the next afternoon when he came home from kindergarten. He was to do it first thing, before he did anything else.

When I paused for breath in my impassioned oration, Jeff responded. "I wish I was a baby again," he said slowly, looking at the floor, "cause when I was a baby, I didn't have to clean up my room." I had to struggle to stifle a smile. At that point in his life, Jeff voiced with a disarming honesty what most of us feel repeatedly in our journey through life.

Somewhere in our pilgrimages, the thought takes shape: Growing up means accepting more and more responsibilities, doing more and more things that once were done for us, making decisions that once were made for us. At how many points in our journeys have we wished for the days when we were taken care of in parental love, when hard choices were made for us?

As a little boy, I probably had some moments like Jeff's plaintive wish. But my clearest and most jolting experience came late, during

my first year in seminary. And it really marked a point of new beginning for me. I was only about a hundred miles from home, but it
might as well have been a thousand. I had no car—and no money
or time to go home if I had had a way to go. I lived across New
Orleans from the seminary campus in the only surviving structure of
the school's former site. One Saturday, I had worked at my regular
job. Then I had nightwatched in a friend's place in order to earn a
few extra dollars. Early on Sunday morning, as I caught the bus to
go across town to my dorm, I realized that I was getting sick. I made
it to my room and to my bed. Barely. For two days, I did what I
knew to do for the flu—I took aspirin, drank orange juice, and
stayed in bed as much as I could. And hundreds of times, I longed
for home, my mother's cool hand on my forehead, her words of
care, and her hot soup. For the first time, on a level of depth, I began to realize that I had moved to a stage in my life where I must
begin to accept more responsibility for myself. Many things that
other people had done for me, I would have to do. And a part of
me wanted to go back.

To have other persons to think and to do for us is easy and comfortable. Many people in our day, adults in age, still want someone
to make decisions for them and to do things for them. They want
their religion to be like that, too. They want tailored answers to their
questions so that they won't have to think or to deal with the hard
questions. They want someone to make decisions and to tell them
what to do. The only problem is that people don't grow that way.
Jeff will grow by assuming more responsibility along the way. So
will I. It isn't easy to think, to choose, to struggle to do a task well.
Often, we may wish for a moment to be back in a less complicated,
less demanding time in our lives. But hopefully for only a fleeting
minute. For the road to maturity is the sometimes hard road of
growing responsibilities, stricter demands, tougher decisions on
which a great deal rides. And it is a road that we travel all of our
lives.

Someone has said that the cherubim and the flaming sword were
placed at the east of the garden of Eden to ensure that Adam and
Eve would not go back to the familiar, the simpler, but would be
forced to go out and on. Just so, we can't go back to our favorite
stretch of life. We must go out and on, meeting new demands as

we make our way. Each stage of life has its own unique challenges, fears, threats, and joys. We must make the most of every stretch of way that we travel.

Lord, sometimes things get so rough and the pressures grow so intense that I find myself wishing I could go back to a simpler stretch in my life. For a moment, I long for less demands, fewer responsibilities, help in making tough decisions — or someone to make them for me. In these moments, go on reminding me that real life is progressive, not static or regressive. Help me not to seek escape but to have the courage, insight, and faith to try, to risk, to go on. May I know the strength that Paul wrote about while he was in prison, the strength that comes from openness to your presence. May I be sufficient for present demands with a sufficiency that comes only from you.

In the name of the One who forged ahead even though the cross loomed in his path, Amen.

On Forgetting People Out

Ye pay tithe of mint and anise and cummin, and have omitted the weightier matters of the law, judgment, mercy, and faith: these ought ye to have done, and not to leave the other undone. (Matthew 23:23)

Are not five sparrows sold for two farthings, and not one of them is forgotten before God?. . . . Fear not therefore: ye are of more value than many sparrows. (Luke 12:6-7)

For God is not unrighteous to forget your work and labor of love. (Hebrews 6:10a)

One day a few years ago, our family was seated at the kitchen table eating lunch—more or less. Our fare was Jeff's number one favorite and high on Leigh's list: hot dogs. We almost were finished when Leigh suddenly exclaimed: "Somebody forgot to give me some potato chips!" Then she looked at me accusingly and said: "Daddy, you forgot me out!"

Leigh's highly indignant protest has stayed with me and has caused me to do some thinking. How often do I "forget people out" in making my way through my days? And deep down, I know that the answer is not what I would like for it to be. I too often forget people out, unintentionally and deliberately. Friends who are close by in terms of distance, who might as well be on the other side of the world for all the thought and time I give to them. Friends from whom I am separated by many miles, with whom I neglect to correspond. People I meet every day, on whom I fail to focus even a few moment's attention. And members of my own family, who need for me to spend part of my time on them alone. I find that forgetting people out is extremely easy.

Sometimes we deliberately close people out. We don't particularly like them. We have nothing at all for them. Often, we have so much going on in ourselves, demanding our mental and emotional energy and our spiritual reserves, that we *can't* share with anyone else at the moment. Much of the time, we are so busy in the pursuit of our own goals, the doing of our business, that we don't make time for other persons. I have the feeling that most of the time, we fail to notice people and their needs because of our preoccupations, our unintentional insensitivity. We find ourselves having to deal with so much and so many, and we must be selective. So, we select some folks out of awareness.

Jesus hit at the proneness to forget out the most significant things in life. He told some religious folks that their tithing on everything that came into their possession was all right, but to omit justice, mercy, and faith was not all right. At least two of the qualities the religious leaders left out had to do with people.

Jesus, on another occasion, indicated that God does not forget out his creatures. The writer of Hebrews reminded his readers that God remembered their works of ministry. God keeps us in the center of his consciousness.

I am trying not to forget Leigh out in our living together as a family. I work at not forgetting out her mother and her brother—and those who ask for a listening ear and an understanding acceptance.

I have an idea that to forget people out is a serious matter to the One who matters supremely.

Lord, too often I am guilty of closing people out. Sometimes, I shut them out because I mean to do so. I don't have time, or something else has priority at the moment. Sometimes, I don't want to relate to those who approach me. Often, I close out those closest to me—and others I encounter—because I am engrossed in my own thoughts or selfish pursuits. I am centered on myself. Help me not to exclude people from my awareness and attention.

I will need your help in becoming less self-centered and more others-centered. Grant me the necessary grace to move toward more of the people I meet.

In the name of him who never forgot out anybody, Amen.

Responsible for Myself

And the Lord God called unto Adam, and said unto him, Where art thou? And he said, I heard thy voice in the garden, and I was afraid, because I was naked; and I hid myself. And he said, Who told thee that thou wast naked? Hast thou eaten of the tree, whereof I commanded thee that thou shouldest not eat? And the man said, The woman whom thou gavest to be with me, she gave me of the tree, and I did eat. And the Lord God said unto the woman, What is this that thou hast done? And the woman said, the serpent beguiled me, and I did eat. (Genesis 3:9-13)

And Nathan said to David, Thou art the man. . . . And David said unto Nathan, I have sinned against the Lord. (2 Samuel 12:7a,13a)

Not too long ago, Jeff went through a stage that paradoxically was humorous and frustrating. Whenever something negative happened to him, he looked around for someone to blame. When he spilled his drink, or dropped food, or fell, his favorite expression to anyone within earshot was an angry accusation: "See what you made me do!"

The humor in most of these situations was that no one had touched him or addressed him in an unusual tone of voice. Often, no one was near him at the moment of his accident. He simply did what we all do now and then: He fumbled, or misstepped, or failed to pay proper attention to what he was doing. Our futile attempts to convince him that we had done nothing to cause his errors were the frustrating element in these scenes. Usually, our attempts to reason and explain logically got us nowhere. Jeff was adamant, unmoved. Someone else had made him commit a bobble.

Hopefully, Jeff will move to the point where he accepts responsibility for what he does, good, and not-so-good. For, too often, I have observed a stark tragedy in myself and people with whom I have dealt. I have discovered that individuals can move to and through adulthood putting blame on everybody and everything else for what they are, what they do, and what they are on the way to becoming. We can go on our way through life, placing blame everywhere except where it actually belongs: on ourselves.

We can blame our parents, who admittedly, at their best, made mistakes with us. We can blame our past or present environment. We never had a chance. We can place the responsibility on a vague, gray mass that we call society. We can single out other individuals who make us do what we do or are the cause of our misfortunes. We even can blame God; his relentless will has dictated what we are, what happens to us, where we are in life, what we have done—or are doing.

When we do something that doesn't fit the image we have of ourselves and try to present to other people, we always can say that we were overcome by the Tempter. Satan is a handy target of our heated charge: "See what you made me do!"

It came as a liberating thought—and as a frightening realization—that *I am responsible for the degree of influence I allow someone or something else to have on me.* I can choose not to be dictated to by my upbringing, my surroundings, my culture, other people, or the devil. I must take responsibility for who I am, what I am becoming, and what I do. At crucial points in my journey, I can make moral decisions which determine my course, choices which change my direction. And I am responsible for those decisions, those choices.

The dialogue in the garden so long ago would be humorous if it were not so serious—and so typical of most of us. When God addressed Adam, Adam said: "Eve made me do it." He even may have said to God: "It's really all your fault; the woman *you* gave me brought the fruit to me, and I ate." When God confronted Eve, she responded: "The serpent made me do it." The hapless snake looked around and had the misfortune of having no one left to blame for his action.

Through Nathan the prophet, God forced the issue with David: "You are the man." Only when we assume responsibility for his actions could healing begin in him. Only when we assume responsibility for ourselves can we move toward wholeness.

I can't look to other people to take care of me. I can't even leave everything to God. Some things—many things—I must do for myself. The other side of the coin is that I cannot evade responsibility for my choices, my actions, or my direction. I am responsible for me.

Lord, it isn't easy for me to assume responsibility for myself. It is easy for me to place blame everywhere but on myself. Thank you for letting me see the great privilege and awesome challenge you have given me: to have a large part in determining the shape of my life. You work creatively in me when I allow you to do so, and I realize that your grace redeemed me and goes on transforming me. These experiences are foundational; I could not and cannot produce them for myself. But there is a lot that I can do for myself that will determine my direction and the quality and productiveness of my life. Help me to be responsible. In the name of him who took his life in hand and never once evaded responsibility for himself, Amen.

The Quality of Courage

Wait on the Lord: be of good courage, and he shall strengthen thine heart: wait, I say, on the Lord. (Psalm 27:14)

Barbara and I had promised Leigh and Jeff that we would take them to Opryland on Labor Day. It would be our last chance to go before the school schedule moved into high gear. Besides, we had not been to Opryland during the summer. The children were excited; I walked through the gates with nagging reservation and dread deep inside. I knew what was coming, and I was not at all sure that I was ready.

We made our way relentlessly toward what to me was an unwelcome test of fatherly fortitude. Leigh had announced that she wanted to ride the Wabash Cannonball twice, once with her mother, and once with me. I did not relish riding a roller coaster that turns one bottom-side-upwards along its winding way. I opted to take Jeff to ride the bump cars while Barbara rode the Cannonball with Leigh. Perhaps one ride would satisfy my adventuresome seven-year-old, and I would be spared.

No such luck. After what seemed to be the twinkling of an eye, Leigh found me hunched down in a too-little car and insisted that I ride with her. With all the enthusiasm of a condemned man trudging the last mile, I started up the ramp with her. We were almost to the top when Leigh said suddenly: "My stomach is trying to make me not do this, but I am." In order to maintain my image as the fearless father, I resisted the urge to tell her that my stomach, in a state of panic and rebellion, had been sending me a few clear, choice messages, too.

I have thought about Leigh's words: "My stomach is trying to make me not do this, but I am." And I have a clear mental picture of her determined face. Other times will come when a sinking feeling in the pit of her stomach will signal the desirability of flight. And those moments may come when the best choice *is* to back off and move away. But she will experience times when determination will overcome a troubled, excited stomach.

We Americans generally hold to a myth that courage is the total lack of fear. Over a long period of time, I have been helped to see that true courage is going on in the face of fear to do what is right, fair, and honorable. To voice an unpopular opinion is not easy. To go against the current, to be a minority of one, to stand up for a conviction may be to invite resistance, difficulty, and anger. We may lose some pseudo friends, become objects of ridicule, or come under threat. Sometimes, all we will have left is an integrity whose strong drive pushes us on despite our fear.

Courage is not the absence of fear; it is going on to do what is right over the protests of an alarmed stomach. And for those of faith, God is the source of courage. He is the One who strengthens the hearts of people so that they go on, even when their stomachs are trying to persuade them to stop—or to turn back.

> Lord, thank you for the emotion of fear that prepares us for fight or flight. It is a good emotion which you put into us for self-preservation. Help me never to ignore the fear that starts to rise from the pit of my stomach. But in those cases where the proper thing to do is to go on in the face of fear, give me courage to act on my convictions. Help me, not so much to calculate the odds against me, but to determine what your spirit, purpose, and desires are. I won't come to the point where I have no fear at all, but I want the determined courage that you alone can give to see something through to the end, even when the cause seems lost.
>
> In the name of the One who completed his mission with courage against overwhelming odds, Amen.

"I Want to Be Like You"

Be ye therefore followers [imitators] of God, as dear children. (Ephesians 5:1)

Be ye followers [imitators] of me, even as I also am of Christ. (1 Corinthians 11:1)

Brethren, be followers [imitators] together of me, and mark them which walk so as ye have us for an ensam-

ple. . . . Those things, which ye have both learned, and
received, and heard, and seen in me, do. (Philippians
3:17a; 4:9)

I had read stories about it and had chuckled. I had heard fathers
talk about it with obvious pleasure. But I really was not quite prepared for the mixed emotions stirred by a small child's words of
pride and awe and love.

Jeff's unprompted words have come on several occasions. Once,
when we were getting ready to attend church services, Jeff asked to
have his vest buttoned exactly like mine. "I just want to be like
you," he said in the open admiration that a child bestows on an
adult as pure gift. Another time, as we were dressing, Jeff suddenly
offered: "When I grow up to be Eli, I am going to have a big T-shirt
like yours." A third time, he wanted a tan dress shirt because, as he
explained to his mother, his daddy had some shirts like that. A
number of times, he has said that he wants to be an editor at The
Sunday School Board—and a railroad engineer like his grand-
father.

In most child-father relationships, the child—especially a boy—
sees his father as a model. He imitates his father in clothing, man-
nerisms, and verbal expressions. And Jeff has reminded me that
being an example, a pattern, and a model for a small child is an
awesome responsibility. Jeff has forced me to ask myself some
searching questions. If he grows up to be like me, what kind of man
will he be? What kind of temperament will he have? From what
kind of attitude—outlook on life, approach to living— will he function? What kind of habits will he cultivate? Will he develop a generous or a miserly spirit because of what he saw and experienced of
my spirit? I won't be responsible for everything he becomes or does.
He will make his own choices as he grows into more and more freedom with its inevitable responsibilities. But I will have some crucial
input. I will model some life-style for him which will have its imprint.

I still can remember wanting to be just like my dad. I ate what he
ate, wanted to be as tall as he was, intended to do his kind of work
when I grew up, and wanted clothes like his. And some of the
things my dad modeled have remained challenges to me: honesty,
hard work, compassion for the underdog, and loyalty in friend-

ships. Deep down, I would like to give Jeff these and other positive options for his living.

I hope Jeff will be a better man because I am his father. Whether or not he *has* more, I pray that he will *be* more—and that he will see clearly that what we are is far more important that what we have or what we do for a living.

Paul had a good grasp of the role of modeling in life. He did not call it that; he called it mimicking. "Mimic God," he wrote; "mimic me even as I mimic Christ," he challenged. We have a supreme spiritual model, and we choose human models. Both play vital roles in our development.

Jeff is, and will continue to be, his own unique self. Hopefully, he will be his own man. But I hope he will receive from me some useful materials as he builds his character. And maybe—just maybe—I will be able to model, to some small degree, the spirit of the One who showed us in clear terms what true, mature humanity is all about. I would like to do that for Jeff and others I encounter along my way. It will be to a lesser extent, to be sure, but it will make a contribution.

> *Lord, it's kind of scary when a small child wants to be like his daddy. I am deeply aware that my children watch me and pick up a lot from me in my unguarded, private moments. I need your help if I am going to offer them an example worth imitating. Even if you enable me to offer them a decent, positive model, I have no guarantee that they will continue to choose to respond. But I want to offer the best that you are able to make me.*
>
> *In the name of him who is the supreme pattern of what you designed people to be, Amen.*

People—or Things?

Thou shalt love thy neighbor as thyself. (Leviticus 19:18b)

But whoso hath this world's good, and seeth his brother have need, and shutteth up his bowels of compassion

*from him, how dwelleth the love of God in him?" (1
John 3:17)*

On that particular Sunday morning, Barbara was not able to
attend worship. Jeff was sick, so she stayed home with him. Leigh
and I had a special father-daughter date: We went to Sunday
School together. I was to preach that morning, which presented a
slight problem—to Leigh, to me, and most assuredly to the saints
who would be called on to endure my preaching. Who would sit
with Leigh during worship? She could be a grown-up, ladylike little
girl when she had the notion, but she needed an adult presence to
render proper cautions when she became the typical, bored, rest-
less seven-year-old. Some friends offered to let Leigh sit with them.
My problem was solved, as was Leigh's. The saints' problem would
remain.

After the worship period, I spoke to some folks and made my
way down to the pastor's study to retrieve some items I had left
there. On my way down the hall, headed for the parking lot, I remembered: Leigh! I turned and started back for the auditorium.
The friend who had sat with Leigh spotted me and said that she was
waiting in the auditorium. I hurried to get her.

"Daddy, you left me." The words were laden with all the indignation that she could muster, which was plenty.

"But I did remember," I responded weakly. "I came back to get
you."

"But why didn't you stay for me? You should have waited." By
this time, we were making our way down a hall toward an exit.

"Well," I replied lamely, "I was thinking about some things I left
in the pastor's study, and I went to get them."

"But Daddy, people are more important than things. Don't you
know that?" The words almost stopped me in my tracks.

The firm statement and the demanding question hung in the air.
Leigh had said what I believe deeply and have tried to preach and
teach consistently. I don't know where she picked up the insight—
from family conversations, Sunday School, kindergarten, or ele-
mentary school. But she had stated the truth as clearly as I had
heard or read it.

People *are* more important than things. Moving to get my daughter was more important than a sermon folder and a book. Stopping to listen, to care, or to help is more important than reading the newspaper, watching television, running some unimportant errand, pursuing some hobby or sport, or obtaining one of our society's trinkets.

Leigh's statement and question have stayed with me. They remind me that my words and deep convictions are worth only as much as my actions. And I have to live with nagging questions: Are people *really* more important than things to me? Is the concept a good idea or a way of life I progressively am making mine? Without doubt, people are worth more than things to the God who made us for himself. And he calls us to his values: people over things. The neighbor. The brother in need or bent low under a heavy load. People matter most of all.

> *Lord, a little child saw it clearly and stated it in simple honesty, the truth that I am prone to forget in my kind of world. I get caught up in a chase after things, and I pass people by, sometimes shouldering past them. Help me to see them, to stop and acknowledge them, to help them when I can.*
>
> *Thank you for counting me to be worth more than things.*
>
> *And thank you for people who bear your image, no matter how faintly.*
>
> *In the name of the One who gave his life for people, Amen.*

The Real Truth

Ye have heard that it hath been said by them of old time, Thou shalt not forswear thyself, but shalt perform unto the Lord thine oaths: but I say unto you, Swear not at all; neither by heaven; for it is God's throne: nor by the earth; for it is his footstool: neither by Jerusalem; for it is the city of the great King. Neither shalt thou swear by thy

head, because thou canst not make one hair white or
black. But let your communication be, Yea, yea; Nay,
nay: for whatsoever is more than these cometh of evil.
(Matthew 5:33-37)

Every family has its own unique expressions which are private,
personal phrases. Our family is no exception. Just like most fathers,
I enjoy kidding with my children. Every so often, I will tease them
with some outlandish, farfetched tale that obviously is fabricated.
Immediately, they challenge me and set about to ferret out the
truth.

On one occasion, Jeff demanded: "Aw, Daddy, tell us the real
truth." He did not accuse me of telling a tale. He just prodded me to
move to the actual facts of the case. Now, when I want to stress that
I am being factual, I often will assure Leigh and Jeff (and sometimes
Barbara) that I am telling "the real truth."

On another occasion, I had asked Jeff a question for which he
had the answer that I needed. He responded, and I checked on his
accuracy. He was right on target. "See, Daddy, I told you the right
truth, didn't I?" he asked, smiling happily. The real truth, the right
truth is composed of words of one person that other people can
count on.

In nonkidding situations, Barbara and I long ago determined that
we would tell Leigh and Jeff the real truth. We would keep our
promises to them, whether the promises had to do with rewards or
punishments. We would try our best to do what we said we would
do so that they would be secure in our words, could count on what
we said.

So, we try to answer our children's questions honestly. Leigh and
Jeff are adopted, and they know that they are. We don't make a big
issue of it, but we tell them as much of what they want to know as
we can. They ask about God, and death, and why people are like
they are sometimes. Often, the easy way would be to sluff off their
questions or to answer in vague generalities. The hard way of the
real, right truth is to be as open, specific, and honest as possible.
Often, the real truth must be phrased, "I don't know," or "I can't do
that." That is difficult honesty, and yet that kind of truth lets our
children see our humanity, our limitations. Maybe it will allow them

to be more comfortable with their humanity, their limitations.

And truth really ought not need embellishment or reinforcement. As Jesus said so well, our yes or no should be enough without the support of swearing. One of the things I want most of all is that Leigh and Jeff—and others whom I meet and who accompany me on my way—will be able to say: "You can count on what he says. He speaks the real truth." I would like for my words to convey the quality of my living. In an age where untruth, half-truths, and fine print are the order of the day, I would like to teach Jeff that the real truth is one of the finest qualities that he can possess and display in his character.

Lord, I haven't always told the real truth—to you, others, or myself. But I really want to do the truth, consistently. Help me to be true and to speak truthfully. I am grateful for all the people who have shown me that open honesty is a real possibility for any individual who sincerely wants to deal above the table in life.

In the name of him who showed us the truth about you and ourselves, Amen.

Recapturing Wonder

When I consider thy heavens, the work of thy fingers, the moon and the stars, which thou hast ordained; what is man, that thou art mindful of him? and the son of man, that thou visitest him? (Psalm 8:3-4)

Leigh had started to the kindergarten that our church provided. Often, I took her in the mornings when I went to my office to begin my day. One day, at lunchtime, she decided that she wanted to walk home with me. The way home wound up a rather steep hill, and I could see myself carrying her the last part of the way. Sometimes, I barely could push myself the last fifty yards of what seemed like straight up. Nevertheless, we started out. And, of course, Leigh walked circles around me.

As we made our way up the hill, Leigh suddenly stopped and

squealed: "Daddy, look!" I looked in the direction she was pointing. I didn't see anything, "Look at the pretty flowers!" she insisted excitedly. Then I saw them: small yellow flowers growing just off the edge of the street. Leigh, at four, still could be struck by the wonder of a small, common flower that we could take to her mother. I was presented with wonder by a child who was teaching me something that I had lost or forgotten somewhere along the way. I still lose it now and then, and my children, in particular, remind me. I must regain periodically the ability to be arrested, grasped by beauty and mystery. My hope is that Leigh and Jeff can retain and refine the art of wonder.

Many of us have lost it, I think, in making our way from childhood to adulthood, and we are the poorer. We so easily lose the art of standing in silent awe before a person, an idea, a song, or a sunset. Beauty, honesty, love, and loyalty—these ought to stop us and bring us up short in amazed celebration. Too often, we neither notice nor care much about the great gifts and qualities of life.

The sad thing is that when wonder is lost, life diminishes. To a wonderless individual, people ceased to be persons and become pawns. The church ceases to be God's redemptive community and becomes another arena where power struggles are fought grimly. Redemption becomes something taken for granted, as though we deserve it. Life becomes a business. Goodness goes unnoticed and unappreciated.

The psalmist looked up at the heavens on a clear night and gazed at the moon and at the stars sprinkled over the dark canopy. He was overcome with awe at God's artistry. I need to recapture a sense of wonder when I encounter virtue, kindness, competence, friendship.

I am glad that I have small children. Perhaps Leigh and Jeff can help me regain the wonder that I see in them, the ability to feel at other times and places what I feel when I look on their sleeping faces. If I can recapture something of wonder at the quality, contributions, and possibilities of some of the people I meet, my life might experience vital rekindlings of hope.

Lord, continue to impress on me the importance of
keeping wonder as a part of life. Help me to see in the

*simple, everyday things and experiences cause for cele-
bration. Give me the capacity to stop and to drink in the
marvelous beauty of people and nature and gracious
acts. Without wonder, I will grow progressively poorer;
with wonder, I never will be poor, even when I don't
have much money.*

*I have an idea that when we pause in wonder at some-
thing or someone in our world, you can and so speak to
us. Keep giving us the sensitivity necessary to stop and to
gaze in awe. In the name of the One who never lost his
sense of wonder at you, your creation, and people,
Amen.*

Getting Darked On

*For thou wilt light my candle: the Lord my God will en-
lighten my darkness. (Psalm 18:28)*

*Deep calleth unto deep at the noise of thy waterspouts:
all thy waves and thy billows are gone over me. Yet the
Lord will command his lovingkindness in the daytime,
and in the night his song shall be with me, and my prayer
unto the God of my life. (Psalm 42:7-8)*

One summer recently, Barbara, the children, and I were visiting
Barbara's folks in Mississippi. We were on vacation, enjoying the
welcome luxury of leisure. Late one afternoon, I was sitting in the
carport reading. A few yards away, in the spacious, fenced-in back-
yard, Leigh and Jeff were playing contentedly. Suddenly, I heard
Jeff address his big sister with a note of seriousness and urgency in
his voice: "Hurry, Leigh. We'd better go inside or we'll get darked
on."

I had heard many descriptions of night's coming, and I had read
some poetic expressions of evening's approach. But I never had
heard night's coming described as getting "darked on." The description from a three-year-old boy's mind remains for me as gra-
phic and profound as it is simple. When day is over and the sun sets

in the west if a person is outside, he or she gets "darked on."

I hope that I can acquaint Jeff with the truth that we all get "darked on" in life repeatedly, in a number of ways. Life's suns have a way of going down too soon, before we are ready. Before we realize it, we are plunged into a long night of waiting anxiously for morning. People turn the lights out on us. Someone hurts us badly, knowingly or unknowingly. People cut us to the quick with words, acts, indifference, or rejection. Something goes wrong physically. The body that has served us so well for so long suddenly develops problems, and accidents that were happening to other people begin to happen to us. And we are faced with our frailty in the awesomeness of ultimates. Cherished relationships end abruptly. Goals are seen clearly as forever beyond reach. The job, career, or profession becomes a dead-end street. Life's suns go down, Jeff. Don't be caught off guard and off balance when they do.

For those of faith, the sun comes up in God's morning. Day follows night; resurrection follows death. Every time. We get "lighted on." Even if things don't come out exactly as we wanted; even if we don't live happily ever after. We may not get what we desire— health, happiness, success, wealth, and longer life—but we will get what God can give. And that is enough.

You *will* get "darked on," Jeff. Count on it. Most likely, you will know some long nights of the soul. But commit your nights to God, who called light into being and who alone can dispel life's deepest darkness. Go on inching ahead, feeling your way in the blackness. You won't make your way alone.

> *Lord, I know what it is to get "darked on." I have had some long nights of the soul, times when I couldn't sing, smile, or feel your presence. I couldn't offer praise to you; I tried to offer my pain. But looking back, I know now that you were there, in the darkness. Perhaps the writer was right; maybe you are a God who lingers in the shadows, not seen but there.*
>
> *I will have other experiences of being "darked on," for I realize that life is more than sunshine and laughter. But help me to hold on to the faith that you are near, that you come to your own, that you share our nights and our*

pain. *And help me to impress this conviction on the children who are gifts from you.*

In the name of the One who, in his darkest night, prayed: "Not as I will, but as thou wilt" (Matt. 26:39), Amen.

Give Daddy Patience

We glory in tribulations also; knowing that tribulation worketh patience; and patience, experience; and experience, hope: and hope maketh not ashamed. (Romans 5:3-5a)

Add to your faith virtue; and to virtue, knowledge; and to knowledge, temperance; and to temperance, patience; and to patience, godliness; and to godliness, brotherly kindness; and to brotherly kindness, charity. (2 Peter 1:5-7)

One evening several years ago, I was trying—with an absolute minimum of success—to serve Leigh and Jeff their suppers with some semblance of smoothness and efficiency. Much more chaos reigned than order. I am convinced that no way has been discovered to feed a four-year-old and an eighteen-month-old in a calm, coordinated manner. I was doing something for Leigh when Jeff, with pronounced gestures and persistent grunts, indicated that he wanted some milk, and right then. Losing my usual unruffled cool for just a fleeting moment, I told him in exasperated tones to hold on for a second. Leigh, in her best big-sister voice, addressed Jeff sternly: "Jeff, give Daddy patience." I froze in midmovement. Of course, she had run together two thoughts: *Give Daddy time,* and *Have patience.* But it came out just right for that particular moment. Her words have haunted me. I recall them from time to time; they have become sort of a prayer for me.

Give me patience—with me. No matter how hard I try, I can't do the things that mean the most to me perfectly, smoothly, and without annoying hitches. Help me to see humor in some of my boners. Help me to laugh at myself so that I will not take myself too seriously or demand the impossible of myself. Help me to learn from painful, embarrassing errors. Let me have something of the patience with me that you have with me.

Give me patience—with the people whose lives bump mine daily. Help me to extend the understanding and the benefit of the doubt to my family, friends, co-workers, and church members that I want from them. Let me not demand too much from other people—more than I demand from myself. Help me to have the patience with them that you have with me.

Give me patience—with you. You don't always do what I want done when I want it done. In fact, a lot of the time you are silent when I ask. And I am left to wonder at the people who seem to have your unlisted number and who receive frequent, clear indications of your will. Help me to have the patience with you that you have with me.

Lord, do give Daddy patience

When We Grow Up

Till we all come in the unity of the faith, and of the knowledge of the Son of God, unto a perfect man, unto the measure of the stature of the fulness of Christ. (Ephesians 4:13)

But grow in grace, and in the knowledge of our Lord and Savior Jesus Christ. (2 Peter 3:18a)

One night a few years ago, Leigh and I were sitting in my favorite chair in the den, enjoying some special time together. She seemed relaxed and comfortable on my lap, and I thought she was engrossed in the television program we were watching. Suddenly, with the disarming directness and simplicity that all four-year-olds seem to possess, she asked: "Daddy, what are you going to be when you grow up?"

With all the coolness and smoothness with which I usually manage to meet her questions, I blurted, "Whaaat?"

She repeated her question with a slightly irritated firmness, emphasizing each word: "I said, *What are you going to be when you grow up?*"

"I thought that's what you said," I replied. After a not-so-dramatic pause, I managed to stammer, "I—I—I—hope to be a reasonably good preacher."

"I wish you'd be a fireman," she responded. Mercifully, the matter ended there, and we went on to other subjects.

Out of the marvelous, mysterious, and magical working of a child's mind came a question not to be dismissed lightly. I have thought a great deal about Leigh's question. I owe her a huge debt of gratitude. What *will* I be when I grow up? For, hopefully, I am growing toward the maturity I desire. I may not be the firefighter that, at that point, Leigh wanted me to be. But I hope that I will be at home in the house of my life so that I will be able to extend real hospitality to other people. I hope that I will be more tolerant, more forgiving, more patient, more open, and more honest. I would like to be able to acknowledge, without embarrassment, the child who still lives in me and let him play at the proper times. I want to be the kind of father whom Leigh and Jeff can acknowledge with pride. I have some ideas about what I want to be when I grow up.

I know a lot of people in chronological adulthood who need to hear—really hear—the direct, simple question: "What are you going to be when you grow up?" To be adult in years and childish in maturity is tragic. To be unaware of not having grown up is even more tragic. If some persons can hear in the question the love and concern that should be there, then they might share a real struggle toward the maturity Paul described as the measure of the stature of the fullness of Christ.

Peter emphasized that we possess the possibility of growing in grace. We can be in the process of maturing spiritually. We can grow to be quality persons who can share grace.

We have something significant to ponder: What are we going to be when we grow up—*if* we grow up?

Lord, continue to give me the constant reminders I need that I am not as mature as I need to be, but a per-

son in the process of growth. I confess that I have those times when, for a fleeting moment, I feel as though I have it all together. But my arrangements of my life have a disconcerting way of coming apart, sometimes flying apart so that some of the pieces are scattered. Help me to continue to work at becoming more mature.

Impress on me when I need it most that growth is the disciplined effort of a lifetime. May I never retire from the struggle to develop toward that maturity which I glimpse in what I know of Christ.

In the name of the One who set the standard and gave us the model for maturity, Amen.

On Liking Who We Are

I will praise thee; for I am fearfully and wonderfully made. (Psalm 139:14a)

One night a few years ago, Barbara and I were bathing the children. After lengthy persuasion, Jeff condescended to give the three of us some "sugar." He planted moist kisses on each of us. Whereupon Leigh, not to be upstaged by her little brother, kissed each of us in turn. And then, with no self-consciousness and without the slightest hesitation, she kissed the back of her hand.

Immediately, I recalled something she customarily did when she was smaller. At night, when one of us tucked her into bed, we would help her list all the people and things she loved. We would thank God for a long list of people—and for Snoopy, her beloved beagle. Somewhere along the way, she invariably would add: "and Leigh."

At that point in her life, Leigh felt good about herself. She found pleasure in her accomplishments: she was happy about her growth; she liked the way she looked and sang and practiced her cheerleading. She had a healthy respect for herself. Now, she takes healthy pride in what she is learning in school, music, and acrobatics. She likes herself.

I hope Leigh can go on feeling good about herself. I intend to do all that I can do to help her. I don't want her to lose something immensely valuable along her way. I don't want her to allow anyone to take it away from her. For I am convinced that many people have lost it, thrown it away, or had it taken from them by insensitive persons. Some individuals have it drummed into them that they really aren't worth much and cannot do enough things well. Some people in our paths feed off of putting others down. Often, these are people who don't feel too good about themselves. We have self-doubts and the tendency to be hard—sometimes too hard—on ourselves. We are prone to interpret imperfection as inferiority. We are unable—or unwilling—to accept our humanity and to go on celebrating life. And, sometimes, with careless or unthinking moves, we throw away a self-respect that is difficult to regain.

Chances are, if people feel good about themselves, they find it easier to feel good about others. If we retain a healthy love for ourselves, we are able to love our neighbors well. If we can keep self-respect and a sense of our value from becoming arrogance, we can see others as having value.

Maybe one reason some of us have so much trouble loving God and people is that we really don't like ourselves much. Until we really accept Christ's acceptance of us as we are and allow him to work creatively in us, we are not likely to love the selves we know ourselves to be.

> *Lord, thank you for the self that I am. I probably would have made me differently if I had had the chance. But you made me a unique person, and you are able to work in me to shape a life that is useful to you.*
>
> *I am incomplete, but with your help I will make progress toward fulfillment. I am imperfect, but I live in the tension created by your demand, "Be . . . perfect" (Matt. 5:48).*
>
> *Help me to retain a sound sense of my self-worth so that I may be able to affirm those in my care and others I meet. Help me to accept my true self, flaws and all, so that I may be able to accept others as they are.*
>
> *In the name of the One who is willing to accept us all, just as we are, Amen.*

6

"I Thank My God upon Every Remembrance of You"
(Philippians 1:3)

Sometimes, unexpectedly, I will remember one of them. For a few moments, I will warm myself with the memory of a quality person whom I knew for a while and who touched my life in a special way. Some of them touched me in passing, and I never saw them again. Some of them were part of my life for substantial periods, making multiple contributions to me. Many of them are gone now. But I live with the knowledge gained from experience that people matter most of all in our journeys.

Not all of the people I have encountered have been pleasant, appealing, or lovely. Some have rejected, hurt, infuriated, frustrated, and dismayed me. Some have used me, dismissed me, or patronized me. These have been a minority. The majority of the people along my path have been fair and open. They may not have invited me to a close relationship, but they allowed me to have my space. They have offered their assistance, and they have extended goodwill.

Both groups—the special people and people of detached goodwill—have allowed me to maintain a basic faith that the goodness of some people out-weighs the ill will, anger, and hostility of others. I have no rosy optimism that insists people are getting better and better naturally. Some persons have responded to Christ so totally that they have his mind, his attitude, or disposition toward life in general and other people in particular. These people remain a constant challenge to me to be the kind of person who helps at least one or two others in their journeys.

An Uncommon Man

And there was not among the children of Israel a goodlier person than he: from his shoulders and upward he was higher than any of the people. (1 Samuel 9:2b)

I heard about him and saw him from distances long before I knew him. I regarded him with the awe only an eleven-year-old boy can feel. His reputation for sternness and exact knowledge of just about everything going on preceded him. So, as a grammar school youngster, I felt the force field of mystery and excitement surrounding L. E. Stewart, math teacher in a small-town school in the deep south.

He was not exactly imposing on first sight. He always seemed to be somewhat rumpled, and his clothes consistently were smudged liberally with chalk dust—the disassembled remains of some recently solved math problem or carefully worked out formula. His light-red, graying hair forever fought a decidedly winning battle with comb and brush. His face was open and friendly, but it could range from radiant good humor to dark foreboding as the occasion demanded. He laughed easily and all over, and he enjoyed sharing a good joke—even when it was on him.

His voice was magnificent. When he started lecturing, all the doors down the halls and around the corners could be heard closing in a vain effort to mute his melon-shaped tones. Deep and strong, his lung power reminded me of a drill sergeant with a company of raw recruits. When raised to its full strength as a prelude to judgment, it caused the most sizable young errant gentleman to cringe. Yet, softened by kindness and genuine care, it gave evidence of a man who possessed a large heart.

He shuffled through the halls and rooms of the little high school, his fastest pace something less than swift; however, he appeared to be everywhere, especially the places where he was least expected by those students plotting—or actively engaged in—mischief. He always seemed to be the first teacher to rumble on the scene of trouble, potential or realized.

Mr. Stewart had been a sailor, a football coach, and a farmer. From the Navy, he had derived his nickname of "Pinky." Two men in his group had had reddish hair. The other man was called "Red." Naturally, Mr. Stewart was tagged with "Pinky." From all his experiences, he brought into the classroom an arsenal of knowledge and methods to use. On occasion, he used anger as a motivating force in mathematics. He was fond of telling us of a test that one of his high school teachers had given him years before (in the bronze age, I was certain), a very unfair test, to his way of thinking. "I got so mad, I decided to show him I could pass any test he could give. I made 98 per cent. If I can make you that mad, I'll do it."

He had a standing offer that never was taken by any student: "If you think you can understand my tests, I'll let you see them before I give them." One look at a sample of his longhand would discourage the best deciphering expert among us. Only he knew what he wrote, and often even his translation was open to serious question. Sometimes, after a few days, he had to guess at the words of a note he had made. After long minutes of inspection, many such notes were deemed unimportant anyway and dismissed. When the class had a chance to vote, some student usually was selected to write formulas, problems, or exams on the chalkboard. He took all this in good humor, and he never changed his writing one scratch or one scrawl.

He was an excellent math teacher, but I remember him even more as a master psychologist. He had much of a boy in him—he had once done most of what would occur to us to do—so students felt comfortable or uncomfortable around him, depending on their past acts or present temptations to err. Not only would students think seriously before doing something questionable, but they felt free to come to him with problems—mostly concerning lagging or fragmenting courtships. Every Monday morning, he was challenged by students who were willing to wager anything that he could not tell them where they were on Saturday night or who was with them. To my knowledge, he never lost a bet. If money had been involved, some challengers still would be paying. Not until we were older did we realize that he always gave the impression that he knew, whether he did or not. This, coupled with shrewd guesses, knowledge of the particular student, and careful listening left the challenger shaking a puzzled head at his mystic insight.

Mr. Stewart was a reasonable, personable man. However, he was never at a loss when reason and friendly persuasion failed. He possessed the fastest belt in the territory. At the first sign of serious trouble, when negotiation broke down, he whipped off his wide belt from his ample middle. In an instant, it was folded and ready. And he never drew unless he meant to do something immediate and remedial. Few ever chose to force the issue. We always waited for his trousers to answer the gentle appeal of gravity when his belt changed from practical implement to persuader; but, evidently, he also was a good judge of his girth, for I do not remember his pants sagging the least bit. Those students unfortunate enough to feel the sting of his belt propelled by strong, farmer's arms spoke with reverence of his power.

Sometimes, he enjoyed projecting a gruff exterior, with his lowered brows forming thunderheads and his cheeks flaming crimson. One of his favorite threats to an inattentive, distracted class was: "I'll give you a nickel to quit and a dime to keep on!" For all his stern discipline and ferociousness, feigned or genuine, he possessed a kind and generous heart. Once, he was giving an exam to some students who had failed a previous one. Since I had passed the first one, he asked me to sit in for him during the test. Some of the fellows asked me to help them with problems, and I did. Later, stricken in conscience, I confessed to him that I had given assistance. With a smile, he placed his hand on my shoulder and said, "Why do you think I asked you to sit in for me?" This bit of unorthodoxy helped me to see more of the man he was.

From this remarkable man, I received my severest punishment, and he never touched me. On a particular exam, several of us were stumped by some of the problems and angered by the test's difficulty. We openly began to pool our intellectual resources. We made no attempt to hide our rationalized "sharing." The next day, Mr. Stewart began the class period by expressing disappointment in some of his students who were not as honest as he had thought. His disappointment was evident in his sagging shoulders, his sad voice, and his tired face. I could not meet his eyes. I had let him down. He was my Sunday School teacher, and I was president of his class. He had called on me to offer public prayer—the first time I remember praying in a crowd—in chapel at school. He had seemed proud of the stumbling, awkward words that I managed to get out. I had not known enough about leading in prayer to stand up when I was called on. I remembered all this that day in class as he talked about cheating. He didn't scold, and he didn't give anybody who "shared" a failing grade. All he did was give me the worst whipping I ever got, and he didn't lay a hand on me. I found myself wishing he had used his belt. In that hour, he used a sensitive situation to teach me a lasting lesson about basic honesty. For all I know, he may have started a boy on the road to becoming a man. He skillfully turned a boy's mistake into an opportunity to teach one of life's finest truths. It remains the only lecture he gave that I still remember.

Mr. Stewart gave me the confidence that somehow started me on the way to believing in myself. The night of the junior class play had arrived. We "players" were having our makeup applied. My face was as white as the powder being used to gray my hair for my role of an aging judge. I never had been so nervous—or more sure of failure. As I sat contemplating my first attempt—and my tragic final attempt, I was certain—to be a star of stage, Mr. Stewart walked in and came over to where I was. "Just relax, son. You'll do a fine job. I know you can do it," he said. I somehow survived without wrecking the play and went on to the same heights of bare survival in the senior class play. I always have been amazed that this man's interest in young lives caused him to say what they needed to begin accepting one of the many challenges that life would give. He knew that high school plays are not of ultimate importance, but he believed that the players were. He gave the encouragement and confidence so important in shaping lives.

The outstanding mark of Mr. Stewart's life, to me, was the consistency with which he lived his days. He was a Christian, a deacon, a Sunday School teacher, a churchgoer—but he was entirely free from false piety. He was the same in the classroom, in the Sunday School room, on the streets, or at a football game. He had captured the secret of living life as a whole instead of segmenting it into the religious and the secular, the occupational and the recreational. His Christianity was evident without his having to sermonize or resort to dramatics to draw attention to it. His faith was expressed through his teaching and living every day. Because he was a Christian, some men and women today are a little better than they would have been had they not studied general math, algebra, or geometry in a small southern high school.

Long ago, a Carpenter spent his short life teaching in a small country. The world was changed forever because of his life. The finest thing that could be said about L. E. Stewart is that he imitated his Master. He spent much of his life teaching in a small school and a small church, but at least one life was shaped to a significant degree by the magnificent way he lived, cared, and gave. That is why I never called him Pinky, and I never will. He always will be Mr. Stewart to me—because of my deep and lasting respect for an uncommon man, a man who stood head and shoulders above most men of his time.

> *Lord, I still remember him with gratitude. I always will. He was a significant person to me during some crucial formative years. He showed me practical Christianity, and he provided a model of a man other than my father. Thank you for the years that I spent under his influence.*
>
> *May his life remain a challenge to me as I live in my children's presence and as I relate to others in their formative years. Enable me to have the positive impact that he had and to offer a quality model of personhood comparable to the one he presented.*
>
> *Help me to be marked by uncommon effort to fill up the pattern that you have given in Christ.*
>
> *In the name of the One who showed us manhood at its finest, Amen.*

Words for the Wilderness

Blessed is the man whose strength is in thee; in whose heart are the ways of them. Who passing through the valley of Baca make it a well; the rain also filleth the pools. (Psalm 84:5-6)

The mouth of a righteous man is a well of life. (Proverbs 10:11a)

I had reached a new low in my life. I had arrived at a desert place that was strange and bewildering. Changes had come too fast for me, and I had not been able to adjust well enough. I was away from home for the first time on an extended basis. I was trying to become accustomed to seminary life. I was living in the largest city I ever had. I was working long hours. I was juggling a full school load, thirty-plus hours of secular work, and a day-long Sunday mission trip to the jumping-off place in Louisiana. I had no breathing space. I felt closed in, loaded down. I was depressed. Really depressed—for the first time in my life.

I wrote home. My dad was away, working in another state with a construction company. So I expressed to my mother my struggle. In a few days, I received an answering letter from her. In it, she wrote that things must be hard for me, and that she understood how tough life could get sometimes. Then, in essence, she encouraged me to keep my chin up and to keep plugging away. I never will forget the gist of the words she wrote next: For many years, she had felt that I would do something fine and important with my life, and she still felt that way; she was certain that I would accomplish something worthwhile.

As I recall the experience now, I reread her words with tears in my eyes. My mother had confidence in me, even when I didn't and when no one else cared much one way or another. My mother never knew how many times I went back to her words in order to gain strength to make my way through the wilderness of depression, to plod along my emotional lowlands.

But don't *all* mothers think that their children are special and destined for great things? Maybe so. I don't know. But what I do know is that *my* mother gave sustaining words for my wilderness when I needed them most. They were the right words at the right time, and they have retained their power across twenty-plus years. They are very much alive in memory.

Life has wilderness stretches for every person. For whatever reason or combination of reasons—physical, mental, or emotional— we find ourselves down, low, and depressed. We suddenly discover that we have a seemingly terminal case of the "blues," the "blahs." The treks through these wildernesses differ in degree of intensity and duration. Things don't look promising. We can't feel good about our prospects for now or tomorrow. When we smile or laugh—if indeed we do—it is an effort or an act.

In the wilderness stretches of our journeys, well-chosen words can make a significant difference. Persons who incarnate Christ's value of individuals can say to others: I have confidence in you. You matter; you count. Whether or not you ever reach one of the world's tallest peaks, you are important because you are here and because you bear God's image.

Words don't solve everything every time. They don't always lead people from their desert places to lands flowing with milk and honey. *But they can.* The possibility always is present. When words are spoken in care and issue from love, then people trudging through barren stretches of their lives can see the green on the horizon. We have an awesome power at our disposal: We can speak redemptive words for people's wildernesses. I know we can. Someone did it for me.

> *Lord, in all the multiplicity of words that I speak, help me to voice some that are redemptive, healing, and creative. I confess that I speak a lot of idle words, wrong words, and angry words. Forgive me. Enable me to be sensitive to the key moments when I can speak words for others' wildernesses.*
>
> *Thank you for those who have helped me to stay upright and moving with their words.*
>
> *In the name of the One who always had—and still has—words for people's wildernesses, Amen.*

A Lesson in Ministry

I was thirsty, and ye gave me drink. (Matthew 25:35b)

The day was typical of New Orleans in the summer: boiling hot with the humidity nudging the top of the scale. At midmorning, I was about halfway through my route and hurrying to finish so that I could have the rest of the day for myself. I was delivering bills for a utility company in an effort to survive as a seminary student. The job paid well, the hours were of my choosing, and I enjoyed the physical activity which served as a welcome contrast to classroom work and outside study.

I was in a rather run-down section of the city—a city of contrasts, mystery, and never-ending interest. I was approaching a rather rickety row of wood-frame apartments whose doors opened onto several wooden steps descending to the sidewalk. I was hot, thirsty, and wet with perspiration.

As I stooped to slide a bill under a screen door into an apartment, I was startled to hear a voice evidently belonging to an elderly black lady. "Would'ja like a glass of water?" she asked.

I was taken by surprise. Today, I can count on the fingers of both hands the number of people who offered me water in six and a half years of delivering utility bills. (And I probably would not need all ten fingers.) On that steaming summer morning, I had a mental picture of murky water in a dirty glass. Too, she was black, and I was white. I politely refused her offer and hurried on my way. Soon, I was away from the wood-frame structure and, then, that section of the city, but I never have gotten away from the encounter.

Only later did I realize fully what had happened. And the more I thought about the incident, the more ashamed I became and the more indelibly the lesson was etched into my life. The nameless, faceless, elderly black woman had done something so scriptural that I had missed it at first: *She had offered to minister out of what she had.* She quite evidently was poor, but she could offer a glass of water to a hot, thirsty man. The fact that I was white did not matter. Although she had no way of knowing what kind of person I was— whether I was "deserving" of what refreshment she could offer— that, too, was unimportant.

The irony of the incident was that as a seminarian, steeped in theology—and destined to be more steeped before I finished—I was preparing to minister to people, and I couldn't recognize real, basic ministry when I walked into it. Too, I had deprived another person of the joy of giving. That lady had a much better grasp of ministry than I had, and I doubt that she could have defined the word *theology*.

My elderly black lady taught me a lesson more vital than anything I learned in a classroom. When you reach out or down to help a fatigued or hurt brother or sister, color, station, or religion do not matter. What matters is offering what you have to another person on the way.

She probably soon forgot the encounter, but I never have. And I never will. She taught a young seminarian that part of being Christ-like is to offer water to the thirsty, that ministry is not just preaching and teaching but being human enough to respond to human need where you find it. It is as simple, and as profound, as that.

Lord, I wince when I remember, but I remember. The lesson will stay with me all of my life. I am grateful for the brief, telling encounter with the caring lady. When I see people who have needs that I can meet, help me to hear again her kind offer. Remind me repeatedly that ministry does not necessarily mean doing great things. In fact, I have an idea it seldom means that. Help me to see that ministry means doing the small, everyday acts of assistance that lie within my ability.

Help me to offer what I have to people with legitimate needs, just as the lady offered water to me long ago.

In the name of the One who spoke of offering cups of cold water to thirsty people, Amen.

A Gift of Time

And they brought young children to him, that he should touch them: and his disciples rebuked those that brought them. But when Jesus saw it, he was much displeased, and said unto them, Suffer the little children to come unto me, and forbid them not; for of such is the kingdom of God. Verily I say unto you, Whosoever shall not receive the kingdom of God as a little child, he shall not enter therein. And he took them up in his arms, put his hands upon them, and blessed them. (Mark 10:13-16)

Mr. Johnny was a retired carpenter who served as custodian—we used the word *janitor*—of our church. He also was a deacon and respected leader in the church. I remember him and his attractive, kind, white-haired wife well. In my mind's eye, I still can see the old car which he drove carefully around our little town. Today, that car would be a valuable antique. Then, it was just old. As a child, I was impressed with the way Mr. Johnny did his work; what he did, he did well.

Each summer, Vacation Bible School came soon after school was out. I didn't particularly like the scheduling. I looked forward to being free for a while after serving my time in the classroom. As soon as possible, I wanted to lose my bad case of schoolroom pallor. But, like a large number of other children of all denominations in our community, I went (usually under parental duress). Mr. Johnny volunteered—or was drafted—for the thankless task of working with active, sometimes rowdy little boys to produce passable handicrafts. He was good with his hands; and, somehow, he managed to help us turn out some usable, attractive objects. Somewhere in the years' accumulation of things in my father's house in Mississippi is a varnished shelf for porcelain figures. Mr. Johnny and I (mostly Mr. Johnny) made it during a Vacation Bible School. I still remember my feeling of pride when I presented the shelf to my mother.

Only after I had grown up and had gone away did I realize what Mr. Johnny had given to me: He had given me the priceless gift of some of his time. He took the gamble. For all he knew, he may have been wasting his time on some ungrateful, insensitive little boys who might throw away what he had worked with them to make. But at least one us—and, I have an idea, a number of us—was helped to realize what he did, what he gave. He gave a small part of himself with great love and patience.

He has been dead for many years, but I think of him every now and then. His influence on at least one person lives on, for I am reminded that one of the greatest gifts that I can give to people close to me and to those people I meet casually is some time to listen, to feel, to respond, and to care. Looking back, I can see a lot of another Carpenter in Mr. Johnny—a Carpenter who always had time for little children and people of all ages who approached him.

Lord, the older I grow the more impressed I become with the extreme value of time. The amount of time I reasonably can expect here is dwindling steadily. I would like to use well whatever I have left. I would like to give some of it in being present to people. Help me to give quality time to my family, doing things with them and for them that will be meaningful to all of us. Help me to give some time to my friends in in-depth sharing as well as occasions of fun. Move me to give some time to other people I encounter on my way, people who are important because they are there and because they ask to be seen and heard.

Most of all, may I devote time to you, your purpose, and your work. Help me to use my time now to prepare me for the moment when time runs out into eternity.

In the name of him who lavished his brief span of time
on people he valued, one at a time, as persons, Amen.

The Prevalence of Grief

Have mercy upon me, O Lord, for I am in trouble: mine
eye is consumed with grief, yea, my soul and my belly.
For my life is spent with grief, and my years with sighing.
(Psalm 31:9-10a)

He is despised and rejected of men; a man of sorrows,
and acquainted with grief: and we hid as it were our faces
from him; he was despised, and we esteemed him not.
(Isaiah 53:3)

She was elderly, limited physically, and alone. She invariably expressed her determination to go home "in a few days." In reality, she probably never left the nursing home. She retained a lively wit She laughed easily. She also cried easily. Some of her memories still were cutting and painful.

The little old lady I visited periodically struggled with her grief, real, insistent, and searing. She had lost so much. Her husband, her sons, her brothers, her home, her health, and her independence—most of what she valued most highly was gone. She talked about it often in an attempt to gain some release from pain deeper than anything physical.

I sat and listened to her. Even after a number of visits, it did not matter to her that I had heard the words many times before. Sometimes, I was extremely uncomfortable. Most *every* time, I was ill at ease. Once or twice, I had to suppress an urge to terminate the visit quickly and leave. Most of the time, I was moved by the intensity of the woman's sorrow. After a while, I understood my uneasiness, my urge to escape. *Her grief got me in touch with mine.* I, too, have suffered losses. Not as many as she, but those I have experienced have been painful. She reminded me that we both dealt with grief and that we are two of an extremely large company.

Any loss produces grief of some degree. The loss of persons dear to us; the loss of friendships; the loss of illusions about people, the church, God; the loss of opportunity, advancement, accomplishment; the loss of youth, health, looks—these and so many more plunge us into a painful struggle with grief. And I am convinced that most of the people I encounter are a lot like me in one respect: They are dealing with grief on some level.

The church as I have experienced it is not what I had thought it to be for so long. For me, the world out there was the arena and the church was a refuge. Then, I found that the churches of my experience were part of the arena. I once was fairly sure that I knew how God acts. Now, more of him is mystery than ever before. I once operated under the assumption that if you dealt openly and aboveboard with people, they would do the same with you. No more. I learned a lesson the hard way. And these losses of what I now recognize to be illusions have produced grief with which I struggle.

I have suffered other—and much deeper—losses. People extremely close to me have died. Friendships have flickered and gone out. Expectations of youth and young adulthood have not been met.

I will encounter grief again down the road. But I will be traveling with One who was "a man of sorrows, and acquainted with grief." He can—and will—share my grief.

My little old lady and I had—and still have, if she lives—a lot in common. And my hunch is that a lot of us have grief in common.

> Lord, I am becoming more and more aware of how large a part grief plays in life. A great deal of the time, I am a grieving person among grieving people. When I lose, help me to work through my grief, recognizing the stages as I go. Help me to come out on the other side stronger, more sensitive to others' grief, and more aware of your presence and resources.
>
> Bless those who struggle with their grief and who have an overwhelming sense of loneliness. Make us, your people, willing to face the risk and threat of sharing others' grief.
>
> In the name of the One who understands grief because he experienced so much of it, Amen.

On Needing People

And the Lord God said, It is not good that the man should be alone; I will make him a help meet for him. (Genesis 2:18)

Only Luke is with me. Take Mark, and bring him with thee: for he is profitable to me for the ministry. (2 Timothy 4:11)

I had sat by her bed in the nursing home for a short while, talking and laughing with her—and listening when I sensed that she was sharing something she wanted heard. Her bed was her home then. Books, magazines, papers, cloths, and various snacks lay next to her on the covers, as neatly arranged as any tidy homemaker's den. She had been in the nursing home for a long stretch of years. She was old and lonely. She was tired and depressed much of the time. And often, she was angry. On that particular day, after we had conversed briefly, we had prayer together. I stood to leave. I told her that I would visit her again.

"Do come back," she said. As I turned to go, she added softly: "I need you."

The words took me by surprise. Whatever the heart strings are, those words caught at mine, got a good hold, and refused to turn loose. "I need you." The words' simplicity and sincerity made them impossible to shake off.

Most of us like to feel needed, to have others see us as adequate, competent, and useful. Not as many of us seem to be fond of admitting that we need other people. Perhaps because of the vastly overrated American myth of rugged individualism and self-sufficient independence. Maybe because to many of us, to need someone else, and to tell them so, is a sign of weakness. I really don't know why we are reluctant to see and to admit our need of other people.

What I do know is that *I* need other people, beginning with the small circle of my family and extending to friends, co-workers, and acquaintances. I need their warmth and their wisdom, their friendship and their faith, their humor and their honesty, their encouragement, and their empathy. Without the sharing of other people, I have found that life becomes a lonely stretch of wilderness.

We need each other—in the church, in the family, in the broad avenues of life's rough and tumble, give and take. If we can recognize this need and admit it, we can begin to move toward each other in openness. We can be persons becoming truly human, and we can begin to celebrate life together.

> *Lord, I have heard those who say, somewhat angrily, that they don't need anybody, that they can make it on their own. I guess I went through a stretch back there when, as a lonely, searching youth I declared that I would reach the point where I didn't need anyone else. Ah, what a fantasy that is. How destitute I would be without all those people who have enriched my life and all those who continue to do so. I am grateful that you have made us for community, fellowship, and friendship. I need people, and I am glad that at least a few people need me.*
>
> *Most of all I—we—need you. Without you, life is a barren wasteland that is forever empty. Continue to meet us at the point of our greatest need.*
>
> *In the name of the One who needed—and still needs—people to share his ministry to a world in desperate need, Amen.*

From Unlikely Sources

Wherefore I put thee in remembrance, that thou stir up the gift of God, which is in thee by the putting on of my hands. (2 Timothy 1:6)

Study to shew thyself approved unto God, a workman that needeth not to be ashamed, rightly dividing the word of truth. (2 Timothy 2:15)

We meet God in the most unexpected places and in the most unlikely people. In common places and events, at the most surprising times, God confronts us with a word we need. Sometimes, we are given comfort or encouragement. At other times, we receive a jolt that causes us to take inventory and to come to a different view of ourselves, our work, and our direction.

I had shared with my home church my decision to enter the pastoral ministry. After a while, my pastor moved. A new man came to our church. He was helpful. He shared some of his experiences, encouraged me, and allowed me to preach for him—although now I know that my "preaching" left a lot to be desired.

I was in the home stretch of my college career, preparing to enter the seminary. One day, the pastor asked if I would like to visit a hospital with him. We went to see a man whom I did not know. He was not a member of our church. During the course of conversation in the hospital room, my pastor mentioned that he was going to be out of town on a Sunday in the near future. He wanted me to preach in his absence. I remember stammering and beating around the bush. I had preached in my home church a number of times. I was pretty well "out of soap." My insecurity was showing.

The patient whom I had just met said something that my inner tape recorder took down, for I still can recall the gist of the man's words: "You're studying to be a preacher, aren't you? You ought to take advantage of every chance you get to preach. It's the only way you'll learn your trade. You'd better take him up on it."

After we left the hospital room, on the way to the car, my pastor told me that the patient was not a professing Christian and that he had been working with the man in an effort to reach him. I wondered then, and I wonder now, what kind of impression an unsure, reluctant preacher made on a man who by outward evidence was not a Christian. But I know one thing: God used him and his words in our brief encounter to say something I needed to hear at that point.

I was much farther along in my journey when I realized that one who tries to proclaim the good news goes on "learning the trade" by gleaning lessons from every effort at proclamation. Too, all any of us can do in this impossible task is to offer what we have. What we offer may not be dynamic or scintillating, but it is all that God asks. And every time we offer the best that we have, we grow; we develop in our role as proclaimers.

And what the hospital patient said to me so many years ago

applies to all who travel the Way. We develop by doing. We grow as ministers by serving in care, sharing what we have. We grow in love by loving, in grace by being gracious, in faith by being faithful to the highest and best we know.

Thank you, Man-whose-name-I-do-not-remember. I met you one time, and in a few words and a few moments, you gave me counsel that God has been able to use in his ongoing work of shaping me.

Lord, continue to confront me and speak to me in surprising places and people. In unexpected moments, give me the challenges and correctives that I need. You know what I really need, even when I am unaware that I have a particular need. Give me the nudgings and the proddings I must have if I am to continue my journey toward the maturity I see in Christ.

Your bringing me up short and presenting a painful lesson that I need to learn is not pleasant. Yet, sometimes it is the only way that you can impress truth on me. Go on supplying my real needs from unlikely sources.

In the name of him who had a knack of seeing expressions of you in the most unlikely people and things, Amen.

Persons of Worth

And they brought young children to him, that he should touch them: and his disciples rebuked those that brought them. But when Jesus saw it, he was much displeased, and said unto them, Suffer the little children to come unto me, and forbid them not: for of such is the kingdom of God. (Mark 10:13-14)

The family moved from Texas to my small Mississippi hometown. The man and his wife were warm, personable people. Their son was two years younger than I but a little bit larger, and we had some things in common. The daughter was quite small. Soon, bunches of children could be seen almost daily, playing in the spacious yard that surrounded the apartment in which they lived.

I enjoyed playing various games in the large "stadium" where we always felt welcome. Football, baseball, volleyball, croquet—we stayed busy with multiple activities. But the thing that surprised and delighted me was the lady's attitude toward the children who came to play at her house. Most of the mothers in our little town did not mind if other children came to play with theirs; but, for the most part, we knew to stay outside. A few mothers would ask us inside, mostly for brief periods. Many ladies of the houses understandably were anxious about what children could do to undo their housekeeping efforts. The lady who had moved from Texas was one of the several who opened their homes to us.

I never will forget the day I discovered that she really liked children, all children it seemed. We were outside, engrossed in a game. Suddenly she called to us and told us to come inside. She actually invited us in! Not only that, she had refreshments ready for us. And, as I recall, she stayed with us and talked with us as though we and what we said really mattered.

Later, when I was much older, I recalled her numerous words and acts, her calling a number of us "her boys," her sympathy and support for the underdogs among us. And I suddenly realized that what impressed me most about her was her relating to the children she met as people who mattered, not as nuisances to be endured or as little people who were relatively insignificant. I recall other grown-ups who were like that, who were warm and hospitable, who opened their homes to us. And I know now that what they did at a difficult stretch of my growing up was to affirm me as a person of worth. Like my lady from Texas, they listened to me, no matter how trivial or naive my statements and questions were. They seemed glad to have me around as their children's playmate.

I'm sorry I took so long to understand what the lady and other people like her have done for me. But often, when I am around some of the little persons I meet along my way, I am reminded of my chance to listen, to talk to them as people of worth, to celebrate their presence. Children are persons of worth. Some people made that truth more than words for me. Perhaps I can do that for my children and for other children I encounter along my way.

Lord, over and over again, in a variety of ways, you have impressed on me the truth that one of the finest things that I can do is to affirm others' worth. All of us need a healthy sense of our value as persons. Some of us have had to struggle to a sound estimate of our worth. Some of us still struggle. In so many ways, we can get indications of our lack of value.

Help us to keep fresh in our thinking your high estimate of our worth, such a high estimate that Christ came and gave himself for us. Then, help us to give our children—all children—a healthy sense of worth. And help us adults to do that for one another.

In the name of him to whom people were and are of ultimate value, Amen.

The Power of Words

A word fitly spoken is like apples of gold in pictures of silver. (Proverbs 25:11)

I had heard the concept put into words many times. I had read about it. I suppose I had preached and taught it. But then the truth was actualized in my experience in such a way that I cannot escape it.

I was somewhere along my way in the undergraduate program in the seminary. I was working at a secular job and studying hard with a view to making it into graduate school. At times, I felt the weight of pressure and frustration—and maybe even some self-pity on the bad days.

One day, I was finishing a meal at the restaurant across the boulevard from the seminary campus. I was eating alone, not always a pleasant experience for me. A graduate student whom I knew mostly by reputation paid for his meal and walked over to my table. I had heard that he had been a promising baseball player until polio ended his career. He was a superior student. I had been told that he finished undergraduate school with the highest grade average in the seminary's history. I looked at him with respect and a degree of awe.

He stopped at my table and greeted me. I responded. Then he said, in essence: "I understand that you are doing quite well in your language courses. Keep up the good work; hang in there with them." I stammered my thanks, and he turned and left the restaurant.

He had no way of knowing what a lift his words gave me. That he would notice, or care, or take the time to say something to me about my studying Greek and Hebrew impressed me. He had taken a moment to encourage someone he did not know, and his simple, brief words had been what I needed at the time. That his words had an impact on me is evidenced by the fact that some twenty-plus years after our encounter, I remember the scene and the essence of his words. Had some people gone out of their way during his hard times to encourage and support him? Had he *not* received the support he needed and out of that experience vowed that he would be an encourager? I don't know. What I do know is that people like him have taught me the power of words to encourage. I am not always the most expressive person in the world, but I have been helped to recognize serious efforts, good work, fine attitudes, and gracious gestures when I see them and to affirm the people who are involved. I have been helped to see that I have at my disposal power to do something positive for people with some well-chosen, timely words.

He paused for only a moment. He spoke only a few words. But he encouraged me at that point in my journey and helped to teach me a truth for a lifetime.

> *Lord, keep me aware of the number of people I encounter every day who are struggling. Some are lonely, or frustrated, or anxious, or under pressure. Some are tired, hopeless, and depressed. Give me the grace to encourage them in rough stretches of their journeys. If all that I can offer are words of concern and support, help me to do that. Thank you for those who have paused in their pursuits to address me in kindness with words of encouragement.*
>
> *In the name of him who always had creative, redemptive words for struggling people, Amen.*

A Way to Repay

Bear ye one another's burdens, and so fulfil the law of Christ. (Galatians 6:2)

But whoso hath this world's good, and seeth his brother have need, and shutteth up his bowels of compassion from him, how dwelleth the love of God in him? (1 John 3:17)

Barbara and I had been in an automobile accident. I had escaped with some bumps and bruises, but she had sustained a back injury. She had to stay in the hospital for two weeks. She was confined to bed for a week at some friends' home and for three weeks at our apartment. When she came home from our friends' house, ladies from the church where I served on staff began to bring meals to the apartment. They checked on Barbara during the day, coming by our apartment or calling. One lady, who with her husband became and remain dear friends, even washed a huge stack of dishes that I had been hoping would go away if I ignored them long enough. This extremely helpful ministry to us by some caring people made possible my carrying out the duties of my work. They helped Barbara to feel secure and less anxious about what needed to be done around the apartment, and they helped to speed her recovery.

One day, I was talking with a lady who had brought food for one of our meals. I expressed my sincere thanks to her for her gift and for others' kindnesses. I had found that cooking a delicious meal was not to be taken for granted. In my unsuccessful attempts to do some simple cooking, I had made some classic messes.

"I don't know how we will ever repay all the gracious things you ladies have done for us," I remember saying, in essence. I fully expected the stock answer: "You don't have to repay us for anything. We don't expect you to pay us back."

"You can't repay us," she said matter-of-factly. Her words surprised me and jarred me for a moment. Then she continued: "But you may have a chance someday to do something like this for someone else. That's all that any of us could ask. That's all the payment I want."

I never have forgotten the gist of that conversation. In a rather normal exchange, an insightful lady had stated a deep principle of living as a genuine human being, as a Christian on pilgrimage. We are to give bread and cups of cold water without expecting something in return. We are to share with those in need with the hope that they will be helped and will be motivated to extend kindness to those they encounter.

Over the course of my life to this point, countless people have given of themselves to me: parents; relatives; teachers in churches and in schools; wife; children; friends; co-workers. All along the way, I have found no means of repaying them in kind. How do you pay someone back for love, kindness, encouragement, care, and generosity with time and effort? I can pay back money or other materials, and I have done so. But I have found that a debt of love, of Christian ministry in care, creates an ongoing tension that constrains me to pass on the kindness that I have received.

A way to repay, at least in part, is to respond to people who have no claims on us just as some compassionate people have responded to us out of no other motivation than to help us a step or two along our way.

> *Lord, so many have done so much for me. You have done so much for me. And, like Paul, I realize that I am a debtor beyond repaying. Yet, I have an idea that you experience something like fulfillment when we love others as you love us, when we give as generously as you have given to us, when we encourage and support as you have strengthened us. The tension is open-ended. That's the genius of it. For we never will be able to reach a point where we can say that we have paid our debt in full. That means that life always must be open to you and to others.*
>
> *Help us to open our lives to you daily, and help us to open our hands to each other.*
>
> *In the name of the One who asks for nothing in return but that we approach each other in love, Amen.*